GREAT SOURCE
Test Achiever

Grade 3

Test preparation for reading, language arts, and mathematics

GReaT SouRCe
EDUCATION GROUP
A Houghton Mifflin Company

Some of the materials in *Great Source Test Achiever* were adapted from *Test Alert*, Level B, by The Riverside Publishing Company.

Design and production by Publicom, Inc., Acton, Massachusetts

Printed in the United States of America

International Standard Book Number: 0-669-46459-7

1 2 3 4 5 6 7 8 9 10 - HS - 03 02 01 00 99 98

URL address:http://www.greatsource.com/

READING: Word Analysis

Directions: Look at the key word. One or more letters are underlined. Find the word that has the same sound as the underlined letter or letters.

1. <u>c</u>ity   tack   sun   corn
          Ⓐ   Ⓑ   Ⓒ

2. <u>sh</u>e   chin   skip   push
          Ⓐ   Ⓑ   Ⓒ

3. r<u>u</u>le   rail   blew   luck   guard
          Ⓐ   Ⓑ   Ⓒ   Ⓓ

4. j<u>oi</u>n   boy   joke   noon   gone
          Ⓐ   Ⓑ   Ⓒ   Ⓓ

Directions: Read the underlined word. Find the word that can be added to it to make a compound word.

5. <u>sun</u>   Ⓐ time   Ⓑ morning   Ⓒ light   Ⓓ bright

6. <u>farm</u>   Ⓐ land   Ⓐ grow   Ⓒ food   Ⓓ milk

Directions: Look at the words. Find the word that has the prefix underlined.

7. Ⓐ camping   Ⓑ <u>re</u>write   Ⓒ <u>c</u>losed   Ⓓ <u>in</u>side

8. Ⓐ <u>de</u>cide   Ⓑ <u>re</u>sting   Ⓒ <u>al</u>ways   Ⓓ <u>un</u>kind

Directions: Look at the words. Find the word that has the suffix underlined.

9. Ⓐ use<u>ful</u>   Ⓑ anim<u>al</u>   Ⓒ s<u>en</u>ding   Ⓓ re<u>port</u>

10. Ⓐ jol<u>ly</u>   Ⓑ mi<u>ster</u>   Ⓒ fair<u>ness</u>   Ⓓ al<u>ike</u>

Pretest

READING: Vocabulary

Directions: Read each sentence. Find the word that means the same, or almost the same, as the underlined word.

11. David is a <u>timid</u> boy.

    Ⓐ handsome

    Ⓑ shy

    Ⓒ clever

    Ⓓ smart

12. The <u>bucket</u> is full of water.

    Ⓐ well

    Ⓑ roof

    Ⓒ truck

    Ⓓ pail

13. Mel came to say <u>farewell</u>.

    Ⓐ hello

    Ⓑ good-bye

    Ⓒ why

    Ⓓ forever

14. The fox quickly <u>vanished</u>.

    Ⓐ disappeared

    Ⓑ raced

    Ⓒ leaped

    Ⓓ hid

Directions: Read each sentence. Find the word that means the OPPOSITE of the underlined word.

15. That color is <u>bright</u>.

    Ⓐ yellow

    Ⓑ dull

    Ⓒ shiny

    Ⓓ light

16. The sign says there is <u>danger</u> ahead.

    Ⓐ safety   Ⓒ traffic

    Ⓑ trouble   Ⓓ stuff

Directions: Read the two sentences. Find the word that best fits the meaning of **both** sentences.

17. Kenny put his beach towel down on the _____.

    Len will _____ the wood to make it smooth.

    Ⓐ deck   Ⓒ shine

    Ⓑ polish   Ⓓ sand

18. Sherry ran across the _____.

    Hannah will _____ the ball.

    Ⓐ table   Ⓒ field

    Ⓑ floor   Ⓓ throw

2

Stop

READING: Comprehension

Directions: Read each passage. Choose the best answer to each question.

Dr. Frederick Fields was a famous heart <u>surgeon</u>. He was very much in demand. No one could have been busier. One day, however, he was approached by a little girl as he left the operating room.

"Please, sir," she said, "will you operate on my doll?"

Without hesitating, Dr. Fields said, "Bring her in here."

In a small side room, he stitched up the doll. No more stuffing would come out now.

"Give her lots of rest for a couple of days," he said to the smiling child. "She'll be just fine."

19. What happened first in this story?

Ⓐ A girl asked Dr. Fields to fix her doll.

Ⓑ The girl took the doll into a side room.

Ⓒ Dr. Fields fixed the doll.

Ⓓ Dr. Fields left the operating room.

20. The passage says that Frederick Fields was a <u>surgeon</u>. A <u>surgeon</u> is a –

Ⓐ doctor

Ⓑ toymaker

Ⓒ farmer

Ⓓ carpenter

21. Why did the doll need to be fixed?

Ⓐ It was very sick.

Ⓑ It did not have a heart.

Ⓒ Its stuffing was falling out.

Ⓓ It was not growing.

22. A good title for this story is –

Ⓐ "How to Fix a Doll"

Ⓑ "The Heart Surgeon with a Heart"

Ⓒ "A Day at the Doll Hospital"

Ⓓ "Dr. Fields's Unusual Hobby"

The Elephant and the Mouse

An elephant and a mouse met in the jungle one day. They were both going in the same direction, so they walked together to pass the time.

After a bit, they came to an old wooden bridge across a river. As they made their way across, the old bridge began to shake and groan and tremble. When they reached the other side, the mouse exclaimed, "We certainly did shake that bridge!"

The startled elephant stared at the boastful mouse but made no reply.

23. What really made the bridge shake?

Ⓐ a strong wind
Ⓑ an earthquake
Ⓒ poor construction
Ⓓ the weight of the elephant

24. At the end, why did the elephant make no reply to the mouse?

Ⓐ The elephant was surprised by the mouse's foolish boast.
Ⓑ The elephant did not hear the mouse.
Ⓒ The elephant was tired of talking.
Ⓓ The elephant didn't know what had made the bridge shake.

25. This story is most like a –

Ⓐ fairy tale
Ⓑ mystery
Ⓒ myth
Ⓓ fable

26. The mouse in the story is most like a person who –

Ⓐ never stops talking
Ⓑ takes credit for what others do
Ⓒ complains about everything
Ⓓ is very good company

27. What happened in this story that could **not** happen in real life?

Ⓐ The mouse walked across a bridge.
Ⓑ The wooden bridge started to shake.
Ⓒ The mouse spoke to the elephant.
Ⓓ The elephant stared at the mouse.

Dear Jessica,

I'm really sorry about what happened at the picnic yesterday. Marcus has never behaved that way before. It must have been the sight of Tessa's cat that made him go wild. He has never liked cats much, but usually he just barks at them.

As soon as he started to leap over the table, I could see that the potato salad would be ruined. And your beautiful crystal bowl! I can't tell you how bad I feel about it. I'll try to find you a new one, but I think that Tessa should help me pay for it. After all, it was her Mitzi that started the whole thing.

Your friend,
Mary Rose

The Owl

Two golden moons that never wink,
Within a feathered hood.
The old owl sits watching me,
Deep in Warlock Wood.
Each night I pass him,
And I say: "Good evening, sir, to you."
Yet every night, forgetful owl
Asks me softly, ". . . Who?"

28. Who is Marcus?

Ⓐ Mary Rose's husband

Ⓑ Mary Rose's son

Ⓒ Mary Rose's dog

Ⓓ Mary Rose's friend

29. What happened to the crystal bowl?

Ⓐ It was washed and returned.

Ⓑ It was overturned and broken.

Ⓒ It was stolen at the picnic.

Ⓓ It was used to feed the cat.

30. Why did Marcus leap over the table?

Ⓐ He wanted some potato salad.

Ⓑ He was playing a game.

Ⓒ He wanted the crystal bowl.

Ⓓ He was chasing a cat.

31. What are the "two golden moons" in the first line of this poem?

Ⓐ the eyes of the owl

Ⓑ the sun and the moon

Ⓒ two stars in the sky

Ⓓ the streetlights

32. The poet jokes that the owl is "forgetful" because the owl –

Ⓐ never winks

Ⓑ forgets his manners

Ⓒ forgets to say "Good evening"

Ⓓ keeps asking "Who?"

Tips for Hikers

Welcome to White Pines Forest. This is one of the most beautiful places in the state. But, it can also be dangerous. If you're planning a hike . . .

1. Wear comfortable shoes or boots, and take along an extra pair of socks. That way you'll have dry socks to change into if you need them.

2. Wear clothing in layers that you can put on and take off. As you walk, you'll probably get warmer. Then you can just peel off a layer or two. Don't forget to carry a waterproof jacket or a rain poncho. The weather can change quickly here.

3. Take some lightweight food along. Dried fruits, nuts, granola bars, and crackers are good energy snacks. Be sure to carry plenty of drinking water. There are no water supplies along the trails.

4. There are some poisonous snakes in the forest, but you can avoid them by sticking to the trails. Remember, the snakes won't bother you if you don't disturb them.

5. Allow yourself enough time to get back to the campground before dark. Pay attention to the trail markings, and you won't get lost.

Happy hiking!

---

33. This passage is mainly about how to –

 Ⓐ have a safe and enjoyable hike

 Ⓑ find the best trails

 Ⓒ avoid poisonous snakes

 Ⓓ choose clothing for a hike

34. Which sentence states an opinion?

 Ⓐ There are some poisonous snakes in the forest.

 Ⓑ There are no water supplies along the trails.

 Ⓒ This is one of the most beautiful places in the state.

 Ⓓ The weather can change quickly here.

35. What is the best reason for hikers to carry extra socks?

 Ⓐ They can use the socks as mittens if the weather turns cold.

 Ⓑ They might get their feet wet.

 Ⓒ They can use the socks for carrying snacks.

 Ⓓ They might get bitten by a snake.

36. The person who wrote these tips mainly wants hikers to –

 Ⓐ be careful

 Ⓑ respect the forest

 Ⓒ eat plenty of food

 Ⓓ be happy

Pretest

LANGUAGE ARTS: Mechanics and Usage

Directions: Read each sentence and look at the underlined word or words. Look for a mistake in capitalization, punctuation, or word usage. If you find a mistake, choose the best way to write the underlined part of the sentence. If there is no mistake, fill in the bubble beside answer D, "Correct as is."

1. Sal <u>growed</u> three inches last year.

   Ⓐ grow
   Ⓑ grown
   Ⓒ grew
   Ⓓ Correct as is

2. <u>Jeff and me</u> went camping.

   Ⓐ Jeff and I
   Ⓑ Him and me
   Ⓒ Jeff and us
   Ⓓ Correct as is

3. Ringo lives in <u>new hampshire</u>.

   Ⓐ New hampshire
   Ⓑ new Hampshire
   Ⓒ New Hampshire
   Ⓓ Correct as is

4. We saw <u>lions tigers and bears</u> at the zoo.

   Ⓐ lions, tigers, and bears
   Ⓑ lions tigers, and bears
   Ⓒ lions, tigers, and bears,
   Ⓓ Correct as is

5. Merle <u>likes</u> to go fishing at Joe's Pond.

   Ⓐ like
   Ⓑ liking
   Ⓒ have liked
   Ⓓ Correct as is

6. Which is the best way to write the beginning of a letter?

   <u>dear mr mason</u>

   Ⓐ dear Mr. Mason,
   Ⓑ Dear Mr. Mason,
   Ⓒ Dear mr. mason,
   Ⓓ Correct as is

7. Jimmy went to <u>dr clay's</u> office.

   Ⓐ Dr Clay's
   Ⓑ Dr. Clays'
   Ⓒ Dr. Clay's
   Ⓓ Correct as is

8. Linda said, <u>"What a nice dog!"</u>

   Ⓐ What a nice dog!
   Ⓑ What a nice dog!"
   Ⓒ "What a nice dog!
   Ⓓ Correct as is

Go On

9. Elizabeth sent me a card on <u>valentine's day</u>.

- (A) Valentine's day
- (B) valentine's Day
- (C) Valentine's Day
- (D) Correct as is

10. Greta hiked <u>farthest</u> than her sister.

- (A) farther
- (B) more far
- (C) more farther
- (D) Correct as is

11. Give the keys to <u>her or I</u>.

- (A) she or I
- (B) she or me
- (C) her or me
- (D) Correct as is

12. The Jacksons have a camp near <u>Harbor Springs, michigan</u>.

- (A) Harbor Springs Michigan
- (B) Harbor springs, Michigan
- (C) Harbor Springs, Michigan
- (D) Correct as is

13. Jeanne is my <u>best</u> friend.

- (A) goodest
- (B) most good
- (C) more better
- (D) Correct as is

Directions: Read the sentences and look at the underlined words. Find the underlined word that has a mistake in spelling. If there are no mistakes in spelling, fill in the bubble beside answer D, "No mistake."

14.
- (A) Gary says he is <u>tired</u>.
- (B) He is <u>goeing</u> home.
- (C) The <u>streets</u> are quiet.
- (D) No mistake

15.
- (A) Jen <u>chose</u> the teams.
- (B) Molly is the best <u>player</u>.
- (C) She <u>desided</u> to pick me.
- (D) No mistake

16.
- (A) Mr. Kean is my <u>neighber</u>.
- (B) He drives an old <u>truck</u>.
- (C) His dogs play <u>together</u>.
- (D) No mistake

17.
- (A) That is a <u>difficult</u> question.
- (B) Did you get the right <u>anser</u>?
- (C) Are you <u>certain</u>?
- (D) No mistake

18.
- (A) The cat <u>scratched</u> the door.
- (B) She wanted to come <u>inside</u>.
- (C) Mom <u>opened</u> the door.
- (D) No mistake

19.
- (A) Stu has many <u>frends</u>.
- (B) <u>Everyone</u> likes him.
- (C) People like him <u>because</u> he is funny.
- (D) No mistake

Go On →

LANGUAGE ARTS: Mechanics and Usage (continued)

Directions: Read each sentence and look at the underlined part. Find the sentence in which the complete subject is underlined.

20. (A) My baby <u>sister</u> can walk by herself now.

(B) She <u>fell and hurt</u> herself yesterday.

(C) <u>My older brother</u> picked her up and hugged her.

(D) She soon <u>stopped crying</u>.

21. (A) <u>Tree toads</u> are very interesting creatures.

(B) Toads do not <u>live in the water</u> as frogs do.

(C) Toads and <u>frogs</u> look almost alike.

(D) My friend <u>Tom</u> caught a bullfrog.

Directions: Read each sentence and look at the underlined part. Find the sentence in which the complete predicate is underlined.

22. (A) <u>Debbie and I</u> go to the baseball field every Saturday.

(B) We <u>practice throwing and catching</u>.

(C) Sometimes we join <u>in a game</u>.

(D) Our team wins <u>most of the time</u>.

23. (A) <u>My favorite season</u> is autumn.

(B) The air is <u>cool and clear</u>.

(C) The leaves on the trees <u>turn</u> colors.

(D) The dry leaves <u>crunch under my feet</u>.

Directions: Find the answer that is a complete sentence written correctly.

24. (A) Vinnie at the barber shop.

(B) For his first haircut.

(C) As the barber lifted his scissors.

(D) Vinnie started crying.

25. (A) Three kinds of fish.

(B) We caught trout, perch, and bass.

(C) Just a fishing line, a hook, and some bread.

(D) We cleaned the fish we cooked them over the fire.

26. (A) We have bins in our garage for recycling.

(B) One bin for cans and one for plastic.

(C) Dad saves newspapers and paper bags he ties them in bundles.

(D) Flattening all of the cardboard boxes.

27. (A) The Pilgrims, a group of people from England.

(B) Landed in America in 1620.

(C) They founded a settlement it was called Plymouth.

(D) They sailed here in a ship called the *Mayflower*.

28. (A) Once upon a time.

(B) The shoemaker was very poor.

(C) Cutting and making shoes.

(D) Two elves helped the shoemaker they made shoes for him.

LANGUAGE ARTS: Composition

Directions: Read each paragraph. Then answer the questions that follow.

> Some names told how people earned a living. Some names suggested where people lived. A person named Farmer was likely to be a farmer. A person named Carver was probably a woodcarver. Mr. Hill probably lived on a hill, while Mrs. Greenwood lived in the forest.

29. Which is the best topic sentence for this paragraph?

Ⓐ My name is Bookman, and I print books.

Ⓑ Pets' names, such as Spot or Snowball, most often describe their looks.

Ⓒ Several hundred years ago, people's last names told something about them.

Ⓓ A man named Meadows probably lived in a grassy area.

30. What is the best way to combine the first two sentences in this paragraph?

Ⓐ Some names told how people earned a living, while others suggested where people lived.

Ⓑ Some names told how people earned a living and where they lived.

Ⓒ Some names told how people earned a living in the places where they lived.

Ⓓ Some names told how people earned a living and lived.

31. What is the main reason this paragraph was written?

Ⓐ to describe the writer's name

Ⓑ to give information about names

Ⓒ to compare names of long ago with names of today

Ⓓ to tell about a man named Farmer

32. Which sentence would fit best at the end of this paragraph?

Ⓐ I know a man named Pinsky whose family came from Russia.

Ⓑ Several hundred years from now, we will not need last names.

Ⓒ Today, two of the most popular names for children are Ashley and Jason.

Ⓓ A family named Castle most likely lived in or near a castle.

Go On →

The chest was full of wonderful things. There was a stone unicorn. It came to life when you touched its horn. Next to it was a pair of silver wings that could take you any place on earth. There was a magic piggy bank that was always full of money. My piggy bank is usually empty. The most special one of all the things was the ruby necklace that could cure any illness.

33. Which is the best topic sentence for this paragraph?

Ⓐ There are many folktales about magical creatures such as unicorns.

Ⓑ I would like to find a chest full of magical things.

Ⓒ When Naomi looked in the cave, she found a treasure chest.

Ⓓ Most chests are made of wood with metal bands.

34. Which sentence does <u>not</u> belong in this paragraph?

Ⓐ Next to it was a pair of silver wings that could take you any place on earth.

Ⓑ There was a magic piggy bank that was always full of money.

Ⓒ My piggy bank is usually empty.

Ⓓ The most special one of all the things was the ruby necklace that could cure any illness.

35. Which is the best way to combine the second and third sentences?

Ⓐ There was a stone unicorn that came to life when you touched its horn.

Ⓑ There was a stone unicorn, but it came to life when you touched its horn.

Ⓒ Although there was a stone unicorn, it came to life when you touched its horn.

Ⓓ There was a stone unicorn, it came to life when you touched its horn.

36. Which is the best way to revise the last sentence?

Ⓐ Most special of all the things in the chest was the ruby necklace that could cure any illness.

Ⓑ The most special thing of all was the ruby necklace that could cure any illness.

Ⓒ Of all the things, the most special thing was the ruby necklace that could cure any illness.

Ⓓ The most special one thing was the ruby necklace that could cure any illness.

Pretest

LANGUAGE ARTS: Reference Materials

Directions: Choose the best answer to each question about finding information.

37. To find information about Thomas Jefferson, you should look in –

(A) a dictionary

(B) an atlas

(C) a magazine

(D) an encyclopedia

38. If you wanted to find out about something that happened yesterday, you should look in –

(A) an encyclopedia

(B) a newspaper

(C) a dictionary

(D) a textbook

39. Look at these guide words from a dictionary page. Which word could be found on the same page?

> frosting – full

(A) fudge

(C) fresh

(B) frogman

(D) fuzzy

40. What would you find on the title page of a book besides the title?

(A) when the book was written

(B) where the author lives

(C) why the book was written

(D) the name of the author

Directions: Use the dictionary entry to answer question 41.

> **hitch** (hich) *Verb* **1.** To fasten, as with a rope, strap, or hook. **2.** To lift or move with a quick jerk. *Noun* **1.** A fastener, such as a *hitch* between a truck and a trailer. **2.** An unexpected delay or problem.

41. Which definition best fits the word *hitch* as it is used in this sentence?

Farmer Jones stopped to *hitch* up his pants.

(A) verb 1

(C) noun 1

(B) verb 2

(D) noun 2

Directions: Use this part of an index to answer question 42.

> plants
>   bushes, 23–28
>   flowers, 34–40
>   shrubs, 19–22
>   vegetables, 41–50
> playgrounds, 82–83
> pottery, 121–124

42. On what pages would you find information about shrubs?

(A) pages 19–22

(B) pages 23–28

(C) pages 34–40

(D) pages 41–50

Stop

Pretest

MATHEMATICS: Concepts and Applications

Directions: Choose the best answer to each question.

1. Which number is 100 more than 3418?

   Ⓐ 4418   Ⓒ 3318

   Ⓑ 3518   Ⓓ 3428

2. Which numeral shows five thousand sixty-two?

   Ⓐ 5620   Ⓒ 5062

   Ⓑ 5602   Ⓓ 5026

3. Which number comes next?

4, 9, 14, 19, ___?___ . . .

   Ⓐ 24   Ⓒ 22

   Ⓑ 22   Ⓓ 20

4. Which number is the arrow pointing to on the number line?

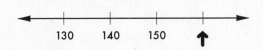

   Ⓐ 120   Ⓒ 155

   Ⓑ 151   Ⓓ 160

5. Which fraction is least?

   Ⓐ $\frac{1}{4}$ Ⓒ $\frac{1}{5}$

   Ⓑ $\frac{1}{3}$ Ⓓ $\frac{1}{8}$

6. What number completes both number sentences?

$$5 + \square = 5 \qquad 3 \times \square = 0$$

   Ⓐ 0   Ⓒ 3

   Ⓑ 1   Ⓓ 5

7. Which number sentence does the picture show?

   Ⓐ $5 - 2 = 3$ Ⓒ $5 + 2 = 7$

   Ⓑ $7 - 2 = 5$ Ⓓ $5 \times 2 = 7$

8. Which fractional part is shaded?

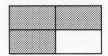

   Ⓐ $\frac{3}{4}$ Ⓒ $\frac{2}{3}$

   Ⓑ $\frac{3}{5}$ Ⓓ $\frac{1}{4}$

9. Which figure is a rectangle?

   Ⓐ   Ⓒ

   Ⓑ   Ⓓ

Go On

10. What is the area of this figure in square units?

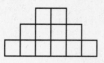

Ⓐ 10 Ⓒ 14

Ⓑ 12 Ⓓ 18

11. How much money is shown?

Ⓐ $0.53 Ⓒ $0.71

Ⓑ $0.66 Ⓓ $0.81

12. What time is shown on the clock?

Ⓐ 1:15 Ⓒ 2:15

Ⓑ 1:30 Ⓓ 3:05

13. About how many units long is the cane?

1 unit

Ⓐ 5 units Ⓒ 10 units

Ⓑ 7 units Ⓓ 15 units

14. Shem left his house at 7:15 A.M. and got to school 15 minutes later. At what time did he get to school?

Ⓐ 7:00 A.M. Ⓒ 7:30 A.M.

Ⓑ 7:20 A.M. Ⓓ 7:45 A.M.

Directions: Solve each problem. If the correct answer is Not Given, mark answer D, "NG."

15. Ms. Carnes bought 3 books for $6.95 each. Which number sentence should you use to find how much she spent in all?

Ⓐ $3 \times \$6.95 = \square$

Ⓑ $\$6.95 - 3 = \square$

Ⓒ $3 \times \square = \$6.95$

Ⓓ $\$6.95 \div 3 = \square$

16. José spent $0.22 for gum and $0.79 for a comic book. <u>About</u> how much did he spend in all?

Ⓐ $0.60 Ⓒ $0.90

Ⓑ $0.80 Ⓓ $1.00

17. Patrick shot 18 arrows at a target. Half of them hit the bull's-eye. How many of the arrows hit the bull's-eye?

Ⓐ 6 Ⓒ 10

Ⓑ 9 Ⓓ 36

18. Margaret is 51 inches tall. She is 4 inches taller than Raymond. How tall is Raymond?

Ⓐ 55 in. Ⓒ 49 in.

Ⓑ 51 in. Ⓓ 47 in.

19. It takes Daphne 39 seconds to swim 1 lap of the pool. Susan can swim a lap in 27 seconds. How much faster than Daphne can Susan swim a lap?

Ⓐ 28 seconds Ⓒ 12 seconds

Ⓑ 13 seconds Ⓓ NG

20. Arnold had 10 CDs in his collection. Charlene had twice as many CDs in her collection. How many CDs did they have altogether?

Ⓐ 20   Ⓒ 40

Ⓑ 25   Ⓓ NG

21. Debra bought an ice-cream cone. She gave the clerk 3 quarters and 1 nickel. She got back 3 pennies as change. How much did Debra's cone cost?

Ⓐ $0.63   Ⓒ $0.83

Ⓑ $0.77   Ⓓ NG

22. In 3 months, Ingrid's sister will be 1 year old. How old is her sister now?

Ⓐ 3 months   Ⓒ 9 months

Ⓑ 6 months   Ⓓ NG

23. Cheryl made 2 dozen raisin cookies. Julio made a half dozen oatmeal cookies. How many cookies did they make in all?

Ⓐ 30 cookies   Ⓒ 20 cookies

Ⓑ 25 cookies   Ⓓ NG

24. Mark has 4 red balls, 5 blue balls, 2 yellow balls, and 8 white balls in a box. If he reaches in and picks 1 ball without looking, what color ball is he most likely to pick?

Ⓐ red   Ⓒ blue

Ⓑ yellow   Ⓓ white

25. Winnie spent $44.95 to buy some shirts. She gave the clerk $50.00. What else do you need to know to find the price of each shirt?

Ⓐ how many shirts she bought

Ⓑ the name of the store

Ⓒ how much change she received

Ⓓ the color of the shirts

Directions: The graph shows the numbers of different kinds of birds seen on a field trip. Use the graph to answer questions 26–28.

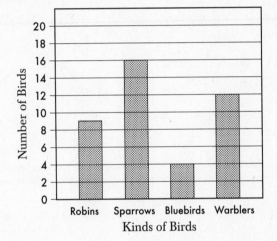

26. How many warblers were seen?

Ⓐ 9   Ⓒ 14

Ⓑ 12   Ⓓ 16

27. Which kind of bird was seen most?

Ⓐ robins   Ⓒ bluebirds

Ⓑ sparrows   Ⓓ warblers

28. How many more sparrows than robins were seen?

Ⓐ 7   Ⓒ 12

Ⓑ 9   Ⓓ 16

MATHEMATICS: Computation

Directions: Find the answer to each problem. If the answer is Not Given, choose answer D, "NG."

29.
$$\begin{array}{r} 87 \\ + 12 \end{array}$$
- Ⓐ 79
- Ⓑ 89
- Ⓒ 99
- Ⓓ NG

30.
$$\begin{array}{r} 285 \\ + 165 \end{array}$$
- Ⓐ 350
- Ⓑ 400
- Ⓒ 550
- Ⓓ NG

31.
$$\begin{array}{r} \$7.88 \\ + 0.21 \end{array}$$
- Ⓐ $7.19
- Ⓑ $8.09
- Ⓒ $8.19
- Ⓓ NG

32.
$$\begin{array}{r} 42 \\ - 19 \end{array}$$
- Ⓐ 11
- Ⓑ 23
- Ⓒ 27
- Ⓓ NG

33.
$$\begin{array}{r} 502 \\ - 83 \end{array}$$
- Ⓐ 439
- Ⓑ 429
- Ⓒ 421
- Ⓓ NG

34.
$$\begin{array}{r} 627 \\ - 235 \end{array}$$
- Ⓐ 347
- Ⓑ 382
- Ⓒ 402
- Ⓓ NG

35.
$$\begin{array}{r} \$41.50 \\ - 33.00 \end{array}$$
- Ⓐ $8.50
- Ⓑ $9.50
- Ⓒ $18.50
- Ⓓ NG

36.
$$\begin{array}{r} 38 \\ \times 6 \end{array}$$
- Ⓐ 128
- Ⓑ 228
- Ⓒ 288
- Ⓓ NG

37. $5 \times 240 =$
- Ⓐ 1200
- Ⓑ 1220
- Ⓒ 1400
- Ⓓ NG

38. 19×4 is closest in value to –

40	60	80	100
Ⓐ	Ⓑ	Ⓒ	Ⓓ

39. $6\overline{)96}$
- Ⓐ 12
- Ⓑ 16
- Ⓒ 18
- Ⓓ NG

40. $4\overline{)27}$
- Ⓐ 6
- Ⓑ 6 R3
- Ⓒ 7
- Ⓓ NG

PRACTICE 1 • Sounds and Letters

Directions: Look at the key word. One or more letters are underlined. Find the word that has the same sound as the underlined letter or letters. Fill in the bubble beside the answer you choose.

SAMPLES

A. mi<u>c</u>e

mine
Ⓐ

came
Ⓑ

sell
Ⓒ

B. h<u>ea</u>d

pet
Ⓐ

team
Ⓑ

deal
Ⓒ

seed
Ⓓ

(**Tips and Reminders**)

- Read each word softly to yourself so you can hear the sounds.

- Watch out for words that have different spellings of the same sounds, as in mi<u>c</u>e and <u>s</u>ell.

- Watch out for words that have the same spelling but different sounds, as in h<u>ea</u>d and t<u>ea</u>m.

PRACTICE

1. <u>b</u>ig

lamb
Ⓐ

robe
Ⓑ

wig
Ⓒ

---

2. <u>c</u>old

king
Ⓐ

race
Ⓑ

sold
Ⓒ

---

3. <u>n</u>ew

grew
Ⓐ

knot
Ⓑ

where
Ⓒ

---

4. <u>j</u>ust

gate
Ⓐ

must
Ⓑ

page
Ⓒ

Go On →

5. r̲ap
 write   tap   while
 Ⓐ   Ⓑ   Ⓒ

6. c̲h̲in
 march   shin   phone
 Ⓐ   Ⓑ   Ⓒ

7. bo̲t̲h̲
 thin   that   batch
 Ⓐ   Ⓑ   Ⓒ

8. s̲top
 listen   whistle   post
 Ⓐ   Ⓑ   Ⓒ

9. m̲i̲ll
 mile   mitt   mail   meal
 Ⓐ   Ⓑ   Ⓒ   Ⓓ

10. e̲arth
 heard   heart   hear   here
 Ⓐ   Ⓑ   Ⓒ   Ⓓ

11. sl̲o̲w
 now   town   tow   claw
 Ⓐ   Ⓑ   Ⓒ   Ⓓ

12. l̲e̲ap
 weigh   wealth   chief   chat
 Ⓐ   Ⓑ   Ⓒ   Ⓓ

13. t̲une
 must   mouse   month   moose
 Ⓐ   Ⓑ   Ⓒ   Ⓓ

14. j̲o̲y
 yoyo   boil   joke   bowl
 Ⓐ   Ⓑ   Ⓒ   Ⓓ

Language Arts

PRACTICE 2 • Grammar and Usage

Directions: Read each sentence and look at the underlined word or words. There may be a mistake in word usage. If you find a mistake, choose the best way to write the underlined part of the sentence. If there is no mistake, fill in the bubble beside answer D, "Correct as is."

SAMPLES

A. Sam <u>plays</u> in the baseball game yesterday.

   Ⓐ play

   Ⓑ played

   Ⓒ playing

   Ⓓ Correct as is

B. <u>Her and I</u> talked on the phone for two hours.

   Ⓐ She and I

   Ⓑ Her and me

   Ⓒ She and me

   Ⓓ Correct as is

C. Trevor and Lindsay <u>like to go</u> horseback riding.

   Ⓐ liking to go

   Ⓑ likes to go

   Ⓒ like to gone

   Ⓓ Correct as is

D. The Mississippi River is <u>more wider</u> than the Snake River.

   Ⓐ widest

   Ⓑ more wide

   Ⓒ wider

   Ⓓ Correct as is

Tips and Reminders

- Try out each answer choice in the sentence to see which one sounds right.

- Be careful with irregular forms of words, such as *felt, grew,* and *went.*

- Watch out for answer choices that are not real words, such as *goed* or *widerest.*

Go On →

PRACTICE

1. Terry <u>gone</u> to the store every afternoon after school.

   Ⓐ go
   Ⓑ going
   Ⓒ goes
   Ⓓ Correct as is

2. <u>Mike and Pat is</u> brothers.

   Ⓐ Mike and Pat are
   Ⓑ Mike and Pat was
   Ⓒ Mike and Pat be
   Ⓓ Correct as is

3. Mina <u>feels</u> ill today.

   Ⓐ feel
   Ⓑ feeling
   Ⓒ are feeling
   Ⓓ Correct as is

4. <u>Him paid me</u> $5.00 for mowing the lawn.

   Ⓐ He paid me
   Ⓑ Him paid I
   Ⓒ His paid me
   Ⓓ Correct as is

5. Mr. Brace gave the leftover muffins <u>to we</u>.

   Ⓐ to ourselves
   Ⓑ to us
   Ⓒ to you and I
   Ⓓ Correct as is

6. <u>Peg and I</u> went to the library on Saturday.

   Ⓐ Peg and me
   Ⓑ I and Peg
   Ⓒ Me and Peg
   Ⓓ Correct as is

7. Jane <u>is tallest</u> than Jean.

   Ⓐ is tall
   Ⓑ is more taller
   Ⓒ is taller
   Ⓓ Correct as is

8. Of all the sled dogs on the team, Lex <u>obeys best</u>.

   Ⓐ obeys better
   Ⓑ obeys goodest
   Ⓒ obeys well
   Ⓓ Correct as is

9. Jake said that <u>he knowed</u> the man, but he did not.

   Ⓐ he knew
   Ⓑ he knowing
   Ⓒ he known
   Ⓓ Correct as is

10. Addie <u>speaks most clearly</u> than her younger brother does.

    Ⓐ speaks more clear
    Ⓑ speaks more clearly
    Ⓒ speaks clearer
    Ⓓ Correct as is

PRACTICE 3 • Whole Number Concepts

Directions: Choose the best answer to each question.

SAMPLES

A. Which number is 10 more than 85?

- Ⓐ 75
- Ⓑ 86
- Ⓒ 95
- Ⓓ 185

B. Which numeral has the greatest value?

- Ⓐ 1004
- Ⓑ 1040
- Ⓒ 1404
- Ⓓ 1044

C. Which is an even number?

- Ⓐ 76
- Ⓑ 57
- Ⓒ 39
- Ⓓ 61

D. What is 312 rounded to the nearest 100?

- Ⓐ 311
- Ⓑ 313
- Ⓒ 310
- Ⓓ 300

Tips and Reminders

- Be sure to look at all the answer choices before you choose an answer. Try each answer choice to find the one that is correct.

- After choosing an answer, read the question again to make sure you have answered it correctly.

PRACTICE

1. Which number is between 807 and 870?

- Ⓐ 871
- Ⓑ 817
- Ⓒ 781
- Ⓓ 718

2. What number is missing?

5, 10, 15, __?__, 25 . . .

- Ⓐ 16
- Ⓑ 19
- Ⓒ 20
- Ⓓ 24

3. Which number shows four thousand two hundred eight?

  Ⓐ 4208

  Ⓑ 4280

  Ⓒ 4028

  Ⓓ 40,208

4. Which number sentence is true?

  Ⓐ 101 > 110

  Ⓑ 127 > 172

  Ⓒ 208 < 198

  Ⓓ 301 > 299

5. Which is fourth in line?

  Ⓐ   Ⓑ   Ⓒ   Ⓓ

6. Which number means 6000 + 10 + 5?

  Ⓐ 615

  Ⓑ 6015

  Ⓒ 6105

  Ⓓ 60,105

7. Which number comes next?

3, 7, 11, 15, ___?___ . . .

  Ⓐ 16

  Ⓑ 17

  Ⓒ 19

  Ⓓ 20

8. What is 966 rounded to the nearest ten?

  Ⓐ 1000

  Ⓑ 970

  Ⓒ 960

  Ⓓ 900

9. Which is an even number?

  Ⓐ 14

  Ⓑ 25

  Ⓒ 37

  Ⓓ 49

10. Which number is the arrow pointing to on the number line?

  Ⓐ 28

  Ⓑ 29

  Ⓒ 30

  Ⓓ 31

11. Which number is 100 less than 3964?

  Ⓐ 3963

  Ⓑ 3064

  Ⓒ 3954

  Ⓓ 3864

12. Which numeral should go in the box?

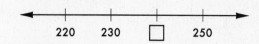

  Ⓐ 231

  Ⓑ 235

  Ⓒ 240

  Ⓓ 250

13. Which number shows ten thousand eighty-five?

Ⓐ 10,850

Ⓑ 10,085

Ⓒ 10,805

Ⓓ 18,050

14. Which number sentence is true?

Ⓐ 703 < 730

Ⓑ 640 > 650

Ⓒ 810 < 801

Ⓓ 515 > 550

15. Which shape comes next in this pattern?

△ △ □ ○ ☆ △ △ □ ○ **?**

Ⓐ △

Ⓑ □

Ⓒ ○

Ⓓ ☆

16. Which number means 2000 + 300 + 30?

Ⓐ 20,303

Ⓑ 20,330

Ⓒ 2330

Ⓓ 2303

17. What is 589 rounded to the nearest 100?

Ⓐ 600

Ⓑ 590

Ⓒ 580

Ⓓ 500

18. Which number is least?

Ⓐ 111

Ⓑ 110

Ⓒ 101

Ⓓ 100

19. Which bird is third from the right?

Ⓐ   Ⓑ   Ⓒ   Ⓓ

20. What number comes next?

6, 8, 10, 12, 14, __?__ . . .

Ⓐ 13

Ⓑ 15

Ⓒ 16

Ⓓ 18

21. Which is an odd number?

Ⓐ 41

Ⓑ 32

Ⓒ 78

Ⓓ 96

22. Which arrow points to 310 on the number line?

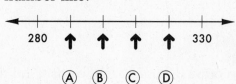

Ⓐ   Ⓑ   Ⓒ   Ⓓ

23

Stop

Reading

PRACTICE 4 • Word Analysis

SAMPLES

Directions: Look at the words. Find the word that has the prefix underlined.

A. Ⓐ res<u>ting</u>
    Ⓑ <u>un</u>like
    Ⓒ <u>ab</u>out
    Ⓓ <u>tw</u>ice

Directions: Look at the words. Find the word that has the suffix underlined.

B. Ⓐ frien<u>ds</u>
    Ⓑ aw<u>ful</u>
    Ⓒ re<u>paint</u>
    Ⓓ near<u>ly</u>

Directions: Find the word that has the root word underlined.

C. Ⓐ <u>cry</u>ing
    Ⓑ ov<u>en</u>
    Ⓒ stay<u>ed</u>
    Ⓓ <u>ball</u>oon

Directions: Read the underlined word. Find the word that can be added to it to make a compound word.

D. <u>air</u>
    Ⓐ climb
    Ⓑ sky
    Ⓒ plane
    Ⓓ clear

> **Tips and Reminders**
>
> - A prefix is added to the beginning of a word, as in *<u>un</u>like*. A suffix is added to the end of a word, as in *near<u>ly</u>*.
>
> - To find a root word, look for a complete word that can stand alone without a prefix, suffix, or other word ending (such as *-s, -ed, -ing, -er, -est*).
>
> - To form a compound word, try each answer choice with the underlined word. Choose the one that sounds right.

PRACTICE

Directions: Look at the words. Find the word that has the prefix underlined.

1. Ⓐ run<u>ner</u>
    Ⓑ <u>no</u>body
    Ⓒ <u>ar</u>ound
    Ⓓ <u>pre</u>cook

2. Ⓐ <u>mis</u>named
    Ⓑ <u>deep</u>er
    Ⓒ <u>col</u>lect
    Ⓓ <u>an</u>swer

3. Ⓐ <u>scr</u>atch
    Ⓑ <u>dis</u>able
    Ⓒ <u>un</u>it
    Ⓓ <u>can</u>dle

Go On

PRACTICE 4 • Word Analysis (continued)

Directions: Look at the words. Find the word that has the suffix underlined.

4. Ⓐ good<u>ness</u>
 Ⓑ cam<u>era</u>
 Ⓒ acr<u>oss</u>
 Ⓓ re<u>make</u>

5. Ⓐ col<u>or</u>
 Ⓑ per<u>form</u>
 Ⓒ pen<u>cil</u>
 Ⓓ neighbor<u>hood</u>

6. Ⓐ seed<u>s</u>
 Ⓑ hope<u>less</u>
 Ⓒ cen<u>ter</u>
 Ⓓ tal<u>ly</u>

Directions: Look at the words. Find the word that has the root word underlined.

7. Ⓐ st<u>ring</u>
 Ⓑ pain<u>ful</u>
 Ⓒ <u>stand</u>ing
 Ⓓ c<u>all</u>er

8. Ⓐ op<u>ened</u>
 Ⓑ sh<u>aking</u>
 Ⓒ happ<u>iness</u>
 Ⓓ dis<u>appear</u>

9. Ⓐ re<u>visit</u>
 Ⓑ <u>change</u>
 Ⓒ fool<u>ed</u>
 Ⓓ <u>less</u>on

Directions: Read the underlined word. Find the word that can be added to it to make a compound word.

10. <u>sand</u> Ⓐ box Ⓑ play Ⓒ pail Ⓓ water

11. <u>up</u> Ⓐ down Ⓑ line Ⓒ stairs Ⓓ house

12. <u>roof</u> Ⓐ house Ⓑ top Ⓒ chimney Ⓓ paint

13. <u>sea</u> Ⓐ beach Ⓑ wave Ⓒ towel Ⓓ shore

14. <u>some</u> Ⓐ one Ⓑ while Ⓒ person Ⓓ week

Language Arts

PRACTICE 5 • Sentences

SAMPLES

Directions: Read each sentence and look at the underlined part. Find the sentence in which the complete subject is underlined.

A. Ⓐ <u>The rain</u> fell all night long.

Ⓑ Strong winds <u>made the house shake</u>.

Ⓒ The <u>power went</u> off at midnight.

Ⓓ We sat <u>in front of the fireplace</u>.

Directions: Find the answer that is a complete sentence written correctly.

B. Ⓐ Two goldfish in the fish tank.

Ⓑ Added a snail and a guppy.

Ⓒ Snails help to keep the tank clean.

Ⓓ Mandy named the snail Slowpoke she named the guppy Pal.

Tips and Reminders

- To find the subject of a sentence, ask yourself *who* or *what* is doing something ("The rain . . ."). The subject is most often a person, place, or thing.

- To find the predicate of a sentence, ask yourself *what* the person or thing is doing (". . . fell all night long."). The predicate is a verb.

- To find the complete sentence, look for the answer that has a subject and a verb and expresses a complete thought. Watch out for answers that include two sentences run together.

PRACTICE

Directions: Read each sentence and look at the underlined part. Find the sentence in which the complete subject is underlined.

1. Ⓐ The flicker is a <u>kind of bird</u>.

Ⓑ <u>The common flicker</u> has a yellow neck.

Ⓒ It is in <u>the woodpecker family</u>.

Ⓓ Flickers eat <u>bugs and worms</u>.

2. Ⓐ <u>Dinah</u> found some shells.

Ⓑ The shells <u>were lying in the sand</u>.

Ⓒ She <u>took the shells home</u> and washed them.

Ⓓ <u>One</u> shell was a clam shell.

Go On

3. (A) On <u>Thursday</u> it snowed all day.
   (B) Marlee called <u>two of her friends</u>.
   (C) She <u>invited them to come over</u> to her house.
   (D) <u>The three girls</u> played games.

Directions: Find the sentence in which the complete predicate is underlined.

4. (A) Fitch <u>was digging in the dirt</u>.
   (B) <u>His shovel</u> hit something hard.
   (C) The thing he hit was a <u>large, white bone</u>.
   (D) Fitch thinks that the bone came <u>from a dinosaur</u>.

5. (A) <u>Two boys</u> walked along the road.
   (B) They heard <u>a loud noise</u>.
   (C) A huge <u>airplane</u> flew over them.
   (D) The boys <u>blocked their ears against the noise</u>.

6. (A) <u>Ms. Blas</u> comes from France.
   (B) France is <u>a large country</u>.
   (C) She <u>speaks French and English</u>.
   (D) Paris is <u>the largest city</u> in France.

Directions: Find the answer that is a complete sentence written correctly.

7. (A) Called the blue whale.
   (B) The largest known mammal in the world.
   (C) Eats tons of food every day.
   (D) A blue whale can grow to a length of 100 feet.

8. (A) Kent went to the library Jake went with him.
   (B) Looked at the kids' videos.
   (C) Jake chose a dinosaur movie.
   (D) Watched the movie three times.

9. (A) Deng Li-Peng lives in a small town in China.
   (B) Grows lots of rice and vegetables.
   (C) Catches fish in the river.
   (D) He works on the family farm he goes to school every day.

10. (A) Making a dream catcher.
    (B) It is made with string and feathers.
    (C) Hangs by the window or near the bed.
    (D) Protects you from bad dreams.

11. (A) Daisies, roses, and many other kinds of flowers.
    (B) Rita weeds the garden she waters the plants.
    (C) Some of the tomatoes will be ready to eat soon.
    (D) Picking and eating peas for the last two weeks.

PRACTICE 6 • Fractions

Directions: Choose the best answer to each question.

SAMPLES

A. Which fraction is shaded?

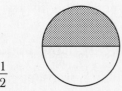

  Ⓐ $\frac{1}{2}$

  Ⓑ $\frac{1}{3}$

  Ⓒ $\frac{1}{4}$

  Ⓓ $\frac{1}{5}$

B. Which fraction is greater than $\frac{1}{2}$?

  Ⓐ $\frac{1}{4}$

  Ⓑ $\frac{1}{5}$

  Ⓒ $\frac{2}{5}$

  Ⓓ $\frac{3}{4}$

Tips and Reminders

- Look at the pictures carefully. Draw your own pictures if that will help you find the answer.

- To compare fractions, change them to "like" fractions with the same denominator.

PRACTICE

1. Which fraction is shaded?

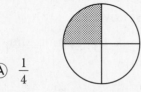

  Ⓐ $\frac{1}{4}$

  Ⓑ $\frac{1}{6}$

  Ⓒ $\frac{1}{3}$

  Ⓓ $\frac{1}{2}$

2. Which fraction is shaded?

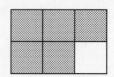

  Ⓐ $\frac{1}{6}$

  Ⓑ $\frac{4}{5}$

  Ⓒ $\frac{5}{6}$

  Ⓓ $\frac{5}{5}$

Go On

3. Which picture shows $\frac{2}{3}$ shaded?

Ⓐ

Ⓑ

Ⓒ

Ⓓ

4. In which group are $\frac{3}{4}$ of the socks shaded?

Ⓐ

Ⓑ

Ⓒ

Ⓓ

5. Which fraction is greater than $\frac{1}{3}$?

Ⓐ $\frac{1}{2}$

Ⓑ $\frac{1}{4}$

Ⓒ $\frac{1}{5}$

Ⓓ $\frac{1}{6}$

6. Which fraction is less than $\frac{2}{5}$?

Ⓐ $\frac{2}{3}$

Ⓑ $\frac{3}{5}$

Ⓒ $\frac{3}{4}$

Ⓓ $\frac{1}{5}$

7. Which fraction is shaded?

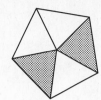

Ⓐ $\frac{2}{5}$

Ⓑ $\frac{3}{4}$

Ⓒ $\frac{2}{3}$

Ⓓ $\frac{3}{5}$

8. Which picture shows $\frac{5}{8}$ of the balls shaded?

Ⓐ

Ⓑ

Ⓒ

Ⓓ

9. Which number sentence is true?

Ⓐ $\frac{1}{4} > \frac{1}{2}$

Ⓑ $\frac{2}{3} > \frac{1}{2}$

Ⓒ $\frac{1}{6} < \frac{1}{8}$

Ⓓ $\frac{3}{4} = \frac{5}{6}$

10. Which number sentence is true?

Ⓐ $\frac{1}{4} > \frac{3}{4}$

Ⓑ $\frac{2}{3} = \frac{1}{3}$

Ⓒ $\frac{2}{6} < \frac{1}{2}$

Ⓓ $\frac{3}{7} < \frac{1}{7}$

PRACTICE 7 • Synonyms and Antonyms

SAMPLES

Directions: Read each sentence. Choose the word that means the same, or almost the same, as the underlined word.

A. Dr. Lopez has a <u>guest</u> in her office.

- (A) problem
- (B) pet
- (C) visitor
- (D) grown-up

Directions: Choose the word that means the OPPOSITE of the underlined word.

B. Jennifer felt <u>ashamed</u>.

- (A) proud
- (B) nervous
- (C) glad
- (D) upset

Tips and Reminders

- Words with the same meaning are *synonyms*. Watch out for answer choices that fit the sentence (such as *problem* and *grown-up*) but have different meanings.

- Words with opposite meanings are *antonyms*. When looking for an antonym, watch out for words that have the same meaning.

PRACTICE

Directions: Read each sentence. Choose the word that means the same, or almost the same, as the underlined word.

1. The police will <u>capture</u> the thief.
   - (A) free
   - (B) catch
   - (C) find
   - (D) question

2. What a <u>foolish</u> thing to say!
   - (A) silly
   - (B) clever
   - (C) wise
   - (D) friendly

3. Gil gave me a <u>present</u>.
   - (A) surprise
   - (B) welcome
   - (C) card
   - (D) gift

4. I have a new catcher's <u>mitt</u>.
   - (A) cap
   - (B) mask
   - (C) glove
   - (D) bat

5. When did the storm <u>occur</u>?

   Ⓐ happen   Ⓒ end

   Ⓑ change   Ⓓ move

6. We had a <u>marvelous</u> time!

   Ⓐ terrible   Ⓒ wonderful

   Ⓑ merry   Ⓓ powerful

7. Our dog likes to <u>roam</u>.

   Ⓐ run   Ⓒ bark

   Ⓑ wander   Ⓓ dig

8. He is a <u>swift</u> runner.

   Ⓐ fast   Ⓒ slim

   Ⓑ tough   Ⓓ slow

9. Kerry is very <u>grateful</u>.

   Ⓐ kind   Ⓒ graceful

   Ⓑ careful   Ⓓ thankful

10. Mom put out the <u>blaze</u>.

   Ⓐ light   Ⓒ oven

   Ⓑ fire   Ⓓ cat

Directions: Choose the word that means the OPPOSITE of the underlined word.

11. That bear is quite <u>tame</u>.

   Ⓐ gentle

   Ⓑ polite

   Ⓒ wild

   Ⓓ strange

12. Jim <u>always</u> calls at five.

   Ⓐ usually

   Ⓑ often

   Ⓒ never

   Ⓓ surely

13. Dad had to <u>punish</u> both of us.

   Ⓐ invite

   Ⓑ reward

   Ⓒ guide

   Ⓓ remind

14. Why are you <u>frowning</u>?

   Ⓐ smiling

   Ⓑ crying

   Ⓒ yelling

   Ⓓ sobbing

15. Nat was <u>discouraged</u>.

   Ⓐ upset

   Ⓑ saddened

   Ⓒ naughty

   Ⓓ hopeful

Stop

Language Arts

PRACTICE 8 • Punctuation

Directions: Read each passage. Some of the sentences contain mistakes in punctuation. Look at each underlined part and decide if it needs to be changed. If it needs editing, choose the best answer. If the underlined part does not need editing, choose answer D, "No change."

SAMPLES

David has trouble getting up in

the <u>morning? As</u> a result, he's often
      A.
late for school. One day <u>he didn't</u>
              B.
<u>get there</u> until nine o'clock.

A.
  Ⓐ morning! As
  Ⓑ morning as
  Ⓒ morning. As
  Ⓓ (No change)

B.
  Ⓐ he didnt get there
  Ⓑ he did'nt get there
  Ⓒ he didn't get they're
  Ⓓ (No change)

> **Tips and Reminders**
> • Check every punctuation mark. Decide if the mark is needed, and make sure it is the right kind of punctuation.
>
> • Read the sentence to yourself to decide if it sounds right. If there is a pause in the sentence, there should be a punctuation mark.

PRACTICE

Carter raised his hand. <u>I can't see</u>
               1.
the blackboard very well," he said.

Our teacher sent him to the nurse's

office. <u>Mrs. Lane gave</u> him an eye
        2.
test. She told him he needed glasses.

1.
  Ⓐ "I can't see
  Ⓑ I cant see
  Ⓒ "I cant see
  Ⓓ (No change)

2.
  Ⓐ Mrs Lane gave
  Ⓑ Mrs, Lane gave
  Ⓒ Mrs' Lane gave
  Ⓓ (No change)

Go On →

121 South Street

<u>Ann Arbor Michigan</u> 48103
3.
<u>July 17. 1997</u>
4.

<u>Dear Lupe.</u>
5.
Yesterday we went hiking and

had a picnic at the lake. Mom

brought <u>sandwiches watermelon,</u>
6.
<u>and cookies.</u> The lake was beautiful.

I wish you had been there with us.

I have missed you this summer.

I'm having a fun vacation, but

<u>it's not the same</u> without you.
7.
<u>Come home soon</u>
8.
<u>Your friend</u>
9.
Carmen

3. Ⓐ Ann Arbor. Michigan
   Ⓑ Ann Arbor, Michigan
   Ⓒ Ann Arbor: Michigan
   Ⓓ (No change)

4. Ⓐ July 17, 1997
   Ⓑ July 17 1997
   Ⓒ July 17! 1997
   Ⓓ (No change)

5. Ⓐ Dear Lupe:
   Ⓑ Dear Lupe!
   Ⓒ Dear Lupe,
   Ⓓ (No change)

6. Ⓐ sandwiches, watermelon, and cookies.
   Ⓑ sandwiches watermelon and cookies.
   Ⓒ sandwiches, watermelon, and cookies?
   Ⓓ (No change)

7. Ⓐ its not the same
   Ⓑ its' not the same
   Ⓒ its'nt the same
   Ⓓ (No change)

8. Ⓐ Come home soon?
   Ⓑ Come home soon,
   Ⓒ Come home soon!
   Ⓓ (No change)

9. Ⓐ Your friend.
   Ⓑ Your friend,
   Ⓒ Your friend;
   Ⓓ (No change)

Stop

PRACTICE 9 • Number Operations

Directions: Choose the best answer to each question.

SAMPLES

A. Which number sentence does the picture show?

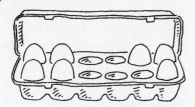

Ⓐ 4 − 3 = 1   Ⓒ 7 − 4 = 3

Ⓑ 4 + 3 = 7   Ⓓ 4 × 3 = 12

B. Which number goes in the box to complete the number sentence?

□ + 12 = 12

Ⓐ 0

Ⓑ 1

Ⓒ 12

Ⓓ 24

Tips and Reminders

• Read each number sentence carefully. Use the pictures to find information.

• Try each answer choice in the number sentence until you find the one that is correct.

PRACTICE

1. Which number sentence goes with the picture?

Ⓐ 3 − 2 = 1

Ⓑ 3 + 2 = 5

Ⓒ 5 − 2 = 3

Ⓓ 2 × 3 = 6

2. Which number sentence goes with the picture?

Ⓐ 6 − 2 = 4

Ⓑ 1 + 6 = 7

Ⓒ 6 − 6 = 0

Ⓓ 2 × 6 = 12

Go On

3. Which sign goes in the circle?

$9 \bigcirc 7 = 2$

+	−	×	÷
Ⓐ	Ⓑ	Ⓒ	Ⓓ

4. Which sign goes in the circle?

$8 \bigcirc 8 = 4 \times 4$

+	−	×	÷
Ⓐ	Ⓑ	Ⓒ	Ⓓ

5. Which number makes this number sentence true?

$20 - 5 = 12 + \square$

Ⓐ 2
Ⓑ 3
Ⓒ 5
Ⓓ 8

6. Which number makes this number sentence true?

$6 \times 4 = 18 + \square$

Ⓐ 3
Ⓑ 4
Ⓒ 5
Ⓓ 6

7. Which number sentence is in the same family of facts as $8 - 3 = 5$?

Ⓐ $3 + 5 = 8$
Ⓑ $8 \times 3 = 24$
Ⓒ $5 - 3 = 2$
Ⓓ $3 \times 5 = 15$

8. What is another way to write 3×7?

Ⓐ $3 + 7$
Ⓑ $7 \times 7 \times 7$
Ⓒ $7 - 3$
Ⓓ $7 + 7 + 7$

9. Which number fits in the boxes to make both number sentences true?

$9 \times \square = \square \times 9$

$\square \times 9 = 9$

0	1	3	9
Ⓐ	Ⓑ	Ⓒ	Ⓓ

10. Which sign goes in the circle?

$32 \bigcirc 0 = 0$

+	−	×	>
Ⓐ	Ⓑ	Ⓒ	Ⓓ

11. What is another way to write $4 + 4 + 4 + 4 + 4$?

Ⓐ $4 + 5$
Ⓑ $4 \times 4 \times 4 \times 4 \times 4$
Ⓒ 4×5
Ⓓ $4 + 4 \times 4$

12. Which number sentence goes with the picture?

Ⓐ $6 - 2 = 4$
Ⓑ $8 - 6 = 2$
Ⓒ $6 \times 2 = 12$
Ⓓ $8 - 2 = 6$

PRACTICE 10 • Context Clues

SAMPLES

Directions: Read the sentence. Find the meaning of the underlined word.

A. More than 200 students sat in the rows of seats in the <u>auditorium</u>. <u>Auditorium</u> means –

   Ⓐ closet   Ⓒ hall

   Ⓑ bus   Ⓓ road

Directions: Choose the word that best completes the sentence.

B. Lisa used some shiny paper to _____ the gift for Laurie.

   Ⓐ wrap   Ⓒ buy

   Ⓑ open   Ⓓ hide

Directions: Read the sentence in the box. Choose the sentence in which the underlined word has the same meaning.

C. | Did you eat a potato <u>chip</u>? |

   Ⓐ Try not to <u>chip</u> my new plate.

   Ⓑ That paint will <u>chip</u>.

   Ⓒ We will all <u>chip</u> in for a gift.

   Ⓓ She gave me one corn <u>chip</u>.

Tips and Reminders

- Use clues in the sentence to decide what the underlined word means.

- Try each answer choice in the sentence to see which one sounds right.

PRACTICE

Directions: Read the sentence. Find the meaning of the underlined word.

1. Mack found the <u>solution</u> to the problem. <u>Solution</u> means –

   Ⓐ result   Ⓒ answer

   Ⓑ ending   Ⓓ beginning

2. Stan was afraid of heights, so he did not even <u>attempt</u> to climb up the rope. <u>Attempt</u> means –

   Ⓐ try   Ⓒ reply

   Ⓑ jump   Ⓓ share

Go On

3. Dad cut the pie into five <u>portions</u> so each of us could have some. <u>Portions</u> means –

Ⓐ dishes   Ⓒ plates

Ⓑ parts   Ⓓ kinds

Directions: Choose the word that best completes each sentence.

Three sisters shared a paper route. They had to __4__ fifty newspapers before school every __5__. Each of the girls rode her __6__ and worked in a different part of the neighborhood.

4. Ⓐ print   Ⓒ read

   Ⓑ send   Ⓓ deliver

5. Ⓐ hour   Ⓒ evening

   Ⓑ morning   Ⓓ time

6. Ⓐ bike   Ⓒ backpack

   Ⓑ pet   Ⓓ wagon

Directions: Read both sentences. Choose the word that best completes the first sentence.

7. Peter picked up the pumpkin and _____ it on the stairs.

Choose the word that suggests Peter was angry.

Ⓐ placed   Ⓒ smashed

Ⓑ set   Ⓓ carved

8. Maggie _____ at me when I walked into the room.

Choose the word that suggests Maggie was pleased.

Ⓐ grinned

Ⓑ stared

Ⓒ frowned

Ⓓ yelled

Directions: Read the sentence in the box. Choose the sentence in which the underlined word has the same meaning.

9. My baby sister is so <u>light</u> that even I can pick her up and hold her.

Ⓐ Please turn off the <u>light</u>.

Ⓑ Did you <u>light</u> the lamp?

Ⓒ The sky was <u>light</u> until nine o'clock last night.

Ⓓ That box of toys is <u>light</u> enough for you to carry.

10. How do birds learn to <u>fly</u>?

Ⓐ John hit a long <u>fly</u> ball.

Ⓑ Sue used a <u>fly</u> to catch the fish.

Ⓒ The plane will <u>fly</u> right over the house.

Ⓓ There is a <u>fly</u> in my soup!

Stop

Language Arts

PRACTICE 11 • Capitalization

Directions: Read the passage and look at the underlined parts. If the underlined part has a mistake in capitalization, find the answer choice that shows correct capitalization. If the underlined part is correct, choose answer D, "Correct as it is."

SAMPLES

(A)   Last week we visited <u>aunt Fay</u>.
     She lives in a small house near
(B) <u>portland, oregon</u>.

A. Ⓐ   aunt fay

 Ⓑ   Aunt Fay

 Ⓒ   Aunt fay

 Ⓓ   Correct as it is

B. Ⓐ   Portland, oregon

 Ⓑ   portland, Oregon

 Ⓒ   Portland, Oregon

 Ⓓ   Correct as it is

> **Tips and Reminders**
>
> • Check every word that has a capital letter. Decide if the word should be capitalized or not.
>
> • Watch for words that should be capitalized but are not, such as the names of people and their titles (*Aunt Fay*) and the names of places (*Portland, Oregon*).

PRACTICE

(1)   My favorite <u>holiday is halloween</u>.
(2) <u>it is a time</u> for costumes and fun and
    trick-or-treating. Halloween comes on
(3) the <u>last day of October</u> every year.

1. Ⓐ   Holiday is halloween

 Ⓑ   holiday is Halloween

 Ⓒ   Holiday is Halloween

 Ⓓ   Correct as it is

2. Ⓐ   It is a time

 Ⓑ   it is a Time

 Ⓒ   It is a Time

 Ⓓ   Correct as it is

3. Ⓐ   Last Day of October

 Ⓑ   last day of october

 Ⓒ   last Day of October

 Ⓓ   Correct as it is

Go On

37 Main Street
(4) Barre, vermont 05641
April 3, 1998

(5) Dear Wendy,
(6)   thanks for the letter you
sent. I especially enjoyed the
(7) story about uncle lou and his
creepy cellar. How did you
ever dare to go down there by
yourself?
        Last week I read a great
(8) book, *make way for ducklings*. It's
(9) about some ducks in Boston,
Massachusetts.
        You should read it when
you have a chance. I think you
would enjoy it.

(10)   fondly,
                Marie Phelps

4. Ⓐ barre, vermont
Ⓑ barre, Vermont
Ⓒ Barre, Vermont
Ⓓ Correct as it is

5. Ⓐ dear Wendy,
Ⓑ Dear wendy,
Ⓒ dear wendy,
Ⓓ Correct as it is

6. Ⓐ Thanks for the letter
Ⓑ Thanks for the Letter
Ⓒ thanks for the Letter
Ⓓ Correct as it is

7. Ⓐ Uncle lou
Ⓑ Uncle Lou
Ⓒ uncle Lou
Ⓓ Correct as it is

8. Ⓐ *Make way for Ducklings*
Ⓑ *make Way for Ducklings*
Ⓒ *Make Way for Ducklings*
Ⓓ Correct as it is

9. Ⓐ Boston, massachusetts
Ⓑ boston, Massachusetts
Ⓒ boston, massachusetts
Ⓓ Correct as it is

10. Ⓐ Fondly,
        Marie Phelps
Ⓑ fondly,
        marie Phelps
Ⓒ Fondly,
        Marie phelps
Ⓓ Correct as it is

Stop

Mathematics

PRACTICE 12 • Geometry

Directions: Choose the best answer to each question.

SAMPLES

A. Which figure is a circle?

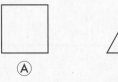

B. What is the area of this figure in square units?

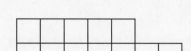

 Ⓐ 6

 Ⓑ 8

 Ⓒ 12

 Ⓓ 16

Tips and Reminders

• Use the pictures to find the information you need.

• After choosing an answer, read the question again to make sure you have answered it correctly.

PRACTICE

1. Which figure is a rectangle?

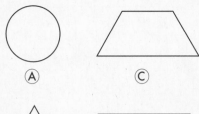

2. How many angles does this figure have?

 Ⓐ 4

 Ⓑ 5

 Ⓒ 6

 Ⓓ 7

Go On →

3. In which pair do the figures have the same size and shape?

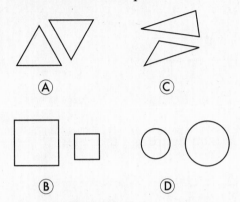

Ⓐ   Ⓒ

Ⓑ   Ⓓ

4. This figure has a missing part. Which shape would fit the missing part exactly?

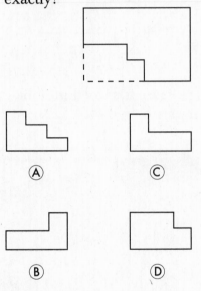

Ⓐ   Ⓒ

Ⓑ   Ⓓ

5. In which figure would the two halves match exactly if the figure were folded on the dotted line?

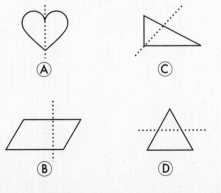

Ⓐ   Ⓒ

Ⓑ   Ⓓ

6. Which is shaped most like a cone?

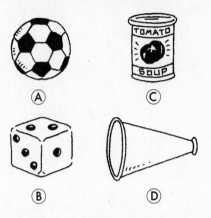

Ⓐ   Ⓒ

Ⓑ   Ⓓ

7. What is the distance around the outside of this figure?

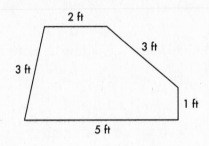

Ⓐ   17 ft   Ⓒ   12 ft

Ⓑ   14 ft   Ⓓ   11 ft

8. What is the perimeter of this rectangle?

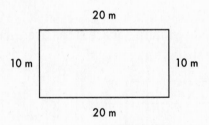

Ⓐ   30 m   Ⓒ   60 m

Ⓑ   50 m   Ⓓ   200 m

9. Which shape appears to be congruent to this figure?

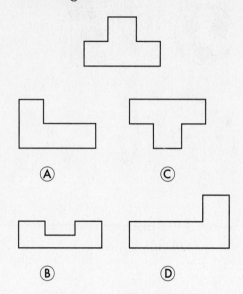

Ⓐ   Ⓒ

Ⓑ   Ⓓ

10. Which shape has a line of symmetry?

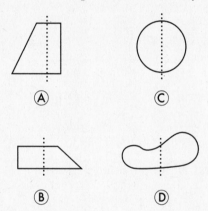

Ⓐ   Ⓒ

Ⓑ   Ⓓ

11. How many square units are there in this figure?

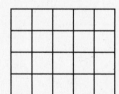

Ⓐ   20
Ⓑ   19
Ⓒ   18
Ⓓ   15

12. What is the area of this figure in square units?

Ⓐ   17
Ⓑ   16
Ⓒ   15
Ⓓ   14

13. Which figure is a triangle?

Ⓐ   Ⓒ

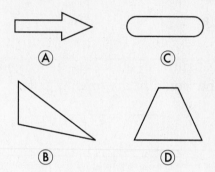

Ⓑ   Ⓓ

14. Which figure is shaped most like a cube?

Ⓐ   Ⓒ

Ⓑ   Ⓓ

PRACTICE 13 • Unfamiliar Words

SAMPLE

Directions: Read the passage. Then answer the questions that follow.

> Mrs. Clark and her son, Jared, went fishing at Foster's Pond. They fished all morning and didn't catch anything. By noon, they were both starving. Jared volunteered to go back to the car to get their lunch. When he returned, he found his mom knee-deep in the pond. She was soaking wet.
>
> "I almost caught a fish this big!" she said, stretching her arms out wide.
>
> "You're pulling my leg, right?" said Jared. "There aren't any fish that big in this pond."
>
> "Well, maybe *you've* never seen one that big," said Mrs. Clark with a chuckle. "But I almost caught one!"

A. In the first paragraph, what does the word "volunteered" mean?

  Ⓐ refused

  Ⓑ tried

  Ⓒ offered

  Ⓓ waited

B. Why does Jared say, "You're pulling my leg"?

  Ⓐ A fish is pulling him into the pond.

  Ⓑ He wanted Mom to catch the fish.

  Ⓒ Something is holding his foot.

  Ⓓ He doesn't believe his mom.

Tips and Reminders

- For words you don't know, look in the passage for clues that can help you guess their meaning.

- If a sentence doesn't seem to make sense the way it is written, look for a "hidden" or implied meaning. Use clues in the passage to help figure out what the sentence really means.

PRACTICE

Directions: Read each passage. Then answer the questions that follow.

Starting your own club can be lots of fun! To help you decide what kind of club to start, think about things you like to do with other kids. Some of those activities might include playing sports, collecting bugs, or helping other people. Pick something you really enjoy.

After you form your club, ask your friends if they would like to join. Ask them to invite some of their other friends to join, too. Don't lose heart if not many kids join your club at first. Maybe they just haven't heard about it yet.

To let people know about your club, make some flyers. Tell the time, date, and place of your next meeting and a little bit about your club. Distribute the flyers to kids in your neighborhood or at your school. Hang in there. Before you know it, lots of people will be asking to join your club. That's when the fun really begins!

1. In the first paragraph, what does the word "activities" mean?

   Ⓐ clubs

   Ⓑ things to do

   Ⓒ jobs

   Ⓓ games to play

2. In the second paragraph, what does "Don't lose heart" mean?

   Ⓐ Don't feel sick.

   Ⓑ Don't get angry.

   Ⓒ Don't get discouraged.

   Ⓓ Don't change your mind.

3. The passage says, "Distribute the flyers to kids." What does "distribute" mean?

   Ⓐ pass out

   Ⓑ collect

   Ⓒ hang up

   Ⓓ print

4. In the last paragraph, "Hang in there" means –

   Ⓐ hang up the phone

   Ⓑ don't give up

   Ⓒ put up some posters

   Ⓓ ask for help

Go On

Bats are the only mammals that can fly. A bat's body is furry like that of a mouse, and it is about the same size. Even though bats may resemble mice with wings, they are not even related to mice. In other words, that "flying mouse" you see at night isn't a mouse at all.

Many bats are nocturnal. They feed at night and sleep during the day. At night, bats use sound instead of sight to find food. As the bat flies around, it sends out high-pitched sounds through its nose and mouth. The sounds bounce off any objects or insects nearby and echo back to the bat. In this way, the bat can tell where its next meal is located.

Although many people believe that bats are blind, the fact is that bats can see, smell, and hear very well. So the next time someone says you are as blind as a bat, you might want to correct him.

5. In the first paragraph, what does "resemble" mean?

   (A) attack

   (B) like to eat

   (C) dislike

   (D) look like

6. The "flying mouse" referred to in the passage is really a —

   (A) bat

   (B) bird

   (C) fly

   (D) mouse

7. Why is it incorrect to say that someone is "as blind as a bat"?

   (A) People are not bats.

   (B) Bats can see very well.

   (C) People can wear glasses.

   (D) People can see at night.

8. The passage says, "Many bats are nocturnal." "Nocturnal" means that bats —

   (A) sleep at night

   (B) are active at night

   (C) love their young

   (D) can't see very well

Go On →

Freddy the Cat was growing old and feeble. Most days he didn't feel like chasing anything. He just wanted to sleep. As a result, the place was crawling with mice. Freddy's owners were talking about bringing in a younger cat to get rid of the mice. Pretty soon they wouldn't need Freddy anymore.

Freddy realized that a younger cat would be bad news for the mice, too. He decided to call a meeting. Curious, the wary mice showed up but made sure they didn't get too close to Freddy. "Who's the big cheese around here?" asked Freddy.

"I am," said Mitch, the mice's leader. "What's this all about?" he asked.

Freddy told Mitch what his owners were planning. They talked for a long time about what to do. They agreed that the mice needed to find a safer place to live.

A few days later all the mice were gone, and everything was back to normal. Freddy yawned. "I may be getting older," he thought, "but I'm still pretty smart." Then he curled up and went back to sleep.

9. In the first paragraph, the word "feeble" means –

   (A) blind

   (B) sleepy

   (C) wise

   (D) weak

10. The passage says, "The place was crawling with mice." This means that –

   (A) the floor seemed to be moving

   (B) there were lots of mice around

   (C) Freddy was so old he could only crawl after the mice

   (D) the mice were chasing Freddy

11. What does Freddy want to know when he asks, "Who's the big cheese around here"?

   (A) which mouse is in charge

   (B) where the mice store their food

   (C) what kind of cheese the mice like to eat

   (D) which mouse eats the most cheese

12. What is the meaning of the word "wary" in the second paragraph?

   (A) lazy

   (B) careful

   (C) angry

   (D) tired

Stop

Language Arts

PRACTICE 14 • Spelling

Directions: Read each sentence. Find the correct spelling of the word that belongs in the sentence.

SAMPLES

A. This _____ jewel almost looks real.

- Ⓐ fak
- Ⓑ fake
- Ⓒ fayk
- Ⓓ faik

B. Use your _____ to cut the paper.

- Ⓐ scissors
- Ⓑ scizzors
- Ⓒ sissors
- Ⓓ sizurs

C. Ouch, I bit my _____!

- Ⓐ tung
- Ⓑ tonge
- Ⓒ tounge
- Ⓓ tongue

Tips and Reminders

- Rule out any answer choices that you know are spelled incorrectly.

- Apply the spelling rules that you know, such as "*i* before *e* except after *c*, or when sounding like *a* as in *neighbor* and *weigh*."

- If you are not sure how to spell a word, look for the answer choice that looks right or that you have seen before.

PRACTICE

1. Tim's family drove to the _____.

- Ⓐ seeshor
- Ⓑ seasure
- Ⓒ seeshur
- Ⓓ seashore

2. Did you _____ the card I sent you?

- Ⓐ recieve
- Ⓑ receive
- Ⓒ reseve
- Ⓓ reseive

3. He was a _____ at the hotel.

- Ⓐ guest
- Ⓑ geust
- Ⓒ gest
- Ⓓ gesst

Go On →

4. Megan put the letter in the _____.

Ⓐ malebox
Ⓑ maleboks
Ⓒ mailbox
Ⓓ mailbocks

5. Use a _____ to slice the cheese.

Ⓐ nife
Ⓑ nyfe
Ⓒ knyf
Ⓓ knife

6. My birthday is in _____.

Ⓐ Jewn
Ⓑ June
Ⓒ Junn
Ⓓ Junne

7. Mica's _____ lives in Maine.

Ⓐ cousin
Ⓑ couson
Ⓒ cuzzin
Ⓓ cuzyn

8. We didn't _____ to see you today.

Ⓐ eckspect
Ⓑ ekspect
Ⓒ expect
Ⓓ expeckt

9. The _____ man didn't like to work.

Ⓐ lasey
Ⓑ lazey
Ⓒ laezy
Ⓓ lazy

10. A _____ stole my bike.

Ⓐ thief
Ⓑ theif
Ⓒ thefe
Ⓓ theef

11. Tina is a very good _____.

Ⓐ stewdent
Ⓑ stuedent
Ⓒ student
Ⓓ studant

12. The _____ children woke up the baby.

Ⓐ noisy
Ⓑ noizy
Ⓒ noisie
Ⓓ noysey

13. The bag is made of _____.

Ⓐ plastic
Ⓑ plastik
Ⓒ plasstik
Ⓓ plastick

14. Who is the _____ of this book?

Ⓐ awthor
Ⓑ awethor
Ⓒ auther
Ⓓ author

15. The teacher asked the children to _____.

Ⓐ behayve
Ⓑ behaiv
Ⓒ behave
Ⓓ behavve

16. Four cups _____ one quart.

Ⓐ equal
Ⓑ eaqual
Ⓒ eqwal
Ⓓ eqewal

17. The necklace was made of _____ stones.

Ⓐ precius
Ⓑ preshus
Ⓒ presious
Ⓓ precious

18. Suzi played a _____ on her piano.

Ⓐ toon
Ⓑ tewn
Ⓒ tune
Ⓓ tunne

Mathematics

PRACTICE 15 • Measurement

Directions: Choose the best answer to each question.

SAMPLES

A. How many inches long is the road from Tom's house to the playground? (Use your inch ruler.)

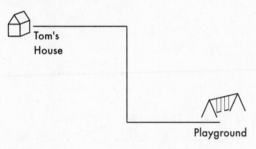

Ⓐ 2 in.   Ⓒ 4 in.

Ⓑ 3 in.   Ⓓ 5 in.

B. When Mia left for the beach, the temperature was 83°F. Which thermometer shows this temperature?

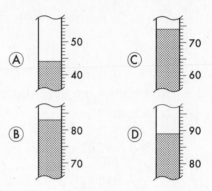

Tips and Reminders

• Use the pictures to find the information you need.

• Make an estimate. Check to see if any of the answer choices is close to your estimate.

• Try each answer choice given. Rule out those that make no sense.

PRACTICE

1. Ted left for school at 7:35. Which clock shows the exact time Ted left for school?

     Ⓐ   Ⓑ   Ⓒ   Ⓓ

Go On

2. Sasha paid 39¢ for a snack. Which of the following shows exactly how much money she paid for the snack?

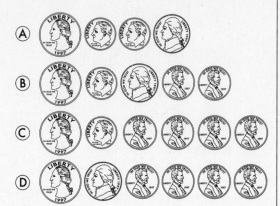

3. Ashley has a piano lesson at 2:15. Which clock shows the exact time of her piano lesson?

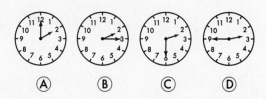

4. Nikki received a $1 bill, a nickel, and a quarter for her allowance. What is the total value of the money she received?

Ⓐ $1.30   Ⓒ $2.05
Ⓑ $1.35   Ⓓ $2.25

5. How many inches long is the road from the Enchanted Forest to the King's Castle? (Use your inch ruler.)

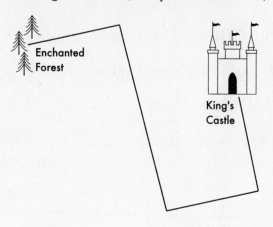

Ⓐ 3 in.   Ⓒ 5 in.
Ⓑ 4 in.   Ⓓ 6 in.

6. Samara is trying to estimate the length of her bicycle. About how long is a bicycle?

Ⓐ 10 in.   Ⓒ 5 ft
Ⓑ 2 ft   Ⓓ 10 ft

7. When Noah went skiing, the temperature was 35°F. Which thermometer shows this temperature?

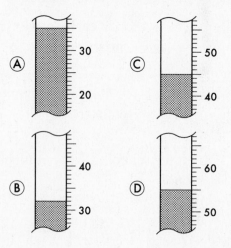

Go On

8. Which unit should you use to measure the distance from one city to another?

Ⓐ centimeters

Ⓑ inches

Ⓒ feet

Ⓓ miles

9. How many centimeters long is the pencil? (Use your centimeter ruler.)

Ⓐ 4 centimeters

Ⓑ 5 centimeters

Ⓒ 6 centimeters

Ⓓ 7 centimeters

10. Ariel ran for 30 minutes. She finished her run at 6:15. Which clock shows the time she started her run?

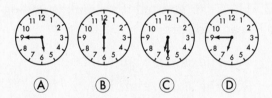

   Ⓐ   Ⓑ   Ⓒ   Ⓓ

11. Aaron took a nickel, a quarter, and a dime from his piggy bank. How much money did he take out of his bank?

Ⓐ 27¢   Ⓒ 40¢

Ⓑ 35¢   Ⓓ 55¢

12. Whose house is closest to the playground?

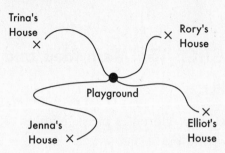

Ⓐ Rory's house

Ⓑ Trina's house

Ⓒ Jenna's house

Ⓓ Elliot's house

13. Which unit should you use to measure the weight of a dog?

Ⓐ ounces

Ⓑ tons

Ⓒ inches

Ⓓ pounds

14. Which thermometer shows the most likely temperature (°F) for a hot summer day?

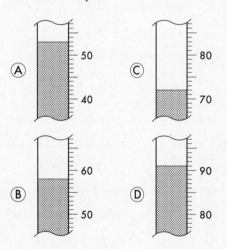

PRACTICE 16 • Main Idea and Details

SAMPLE

Directions: Here is a passage about skunks. Read the passage. Then answer the questions.

> Most people will do everything they can to avoid skunks. That's because skunks have a secret weapon. They make a really smelly liquid called musk that they can spray at people or animals up to 15 feet away. The bad news for people is that skunks also have a great aim!
>
> The good news is the skunk will spray only if it has to and only after it has tried to warn you. The last warning is usually when the skunk raises its tail. That's where the musk is stored (in two small sacs under the skunk's tail). So, if you come across a skunk with its tail raised, run the other way!

A. Which is the best title for this passage?

  Ⓐ "People Beware!"

  Ⓑ "How Skunks Hunt"

  Ⓒ "The Smelly Truth About Skunks"

  Ⓓ "The Striped Cat"

B. How can you tell if a skunk is getting ready to spray?

  Ⓐ The skunk's tail is raised.

  Ⓑ The skunk aims its nose at something.

  Ⓒ The skunk smells bad.

  Ⓓ The skunk runs after you.

Tips and Reminders

- Scan the questions quickly to see what you should look for in the passage.

- Read the whole passage carefully. To find the main idea or main topic, decide what the whole passage is mostly about.

- To find details, look back at the passage.

- Try to answer the question before looking at the answer choices. Check to see if your answer is one of the choices.

Go On

PRACTICE

Directions: More goes on under the water in a lake than most people realize. To get a closer look, read these directions for building a "waterscope." Then answer questions 1–4.

You'll need:
- a plastic knife
- a large plastic container
- some clear plastic wrap
- a strong rubber band

Here's what you do:
1. Use the plastic knife to cut out the bottom of the container.
2. Stretch plastic wrap across the bottom of the container. Make sure it is stretched tight.
3. Use a rubber band to hold the plastic wrap in place.

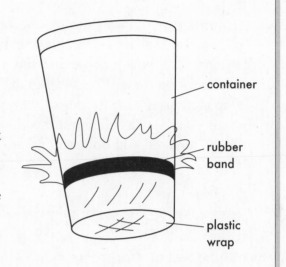

Bring your waterscope to the lake. Paddle a boat or raft over to a shallow marsh. Push your waterscope down into the water and look in. What you see will amaze you!

1. Which is the best title for this passage?

  Ⓐ "How to Have Fun at the Lake"
  Ⓑ "Making a Waterscope"
  Ⓒ "Spying at the Lake"
  Ⓓ "Life Under the Water"

2. The rubber band is used to

  Ⓐ keep the water out
  Ⓑ cut the container
  Ⓒ hold the plastic wrap in place
  Ⓓ make a lid for the container

3. This passage is mostly about

  Ⓐ how to build a waterscope
  Ⓑ how to paddle a boat on the lake
  Ⓒ what goes on underwater at a lake
  Ⓓ cutting a container

4. To make a waterscope, you will need a

  Ⓐ shallow marsh
  Ⓑ plastic container
  Ⓒ paddle
  Ⓓ boat or raft

Go On

Directions: Here is a story about two brothers. Read the story to find out what happens to them. Then answer questions 5–8.

"Can I borrow your watch?" Timmy asked his brother.

"Only if you promise to take very good care of it," said Ethan. Timmy promised, and Ethan let him have the watch. "Just for today," Ethan said.

Timmy wore the watch to his soccer game. Before the game he took it off and put it down on the players' bench. Then he forgot all about the watch until he got home and saw Ethan.

"Where's my watch?" asked Ethan. Timmy didn't know what to say. He opened his mouth to speak, but no words came out. Ethan reached into his pocket and pulled out the watch.

"Hey, how did you do that?" asked Timmy.

"Easy," said Ethan. "Your soccer coach just stopped by and dropped it off."

---

5. Which is the best title for this story?

Ⓐ "Finders Keepers"

Ⓑ "The Lost Watch"

Ⓒ "Timmy's Soccer Game"

Ⓓ "Learning to Share"

6. Ethan let Timmy borrow his watch because Timmy promised to

Ⓐ wear it to the soccer game

Ⓑ give it to his soccer coach

Ⓒ take very good care of it

Ⓓ buy him a new one

7. What did Timmy do with the watch after he took it off?

Ⓐ He put it on the players' bench.

Ⓑ He gave it to his coach.

Ⓒ He put it in his pocket.

Ⓓ He gave it to his brother.

8. What is the main idea of this passage?

Ⓐ Ethan played a trick on his brother.

Ⓑ Timmy borrowed his brother's watch and lost it.

Ⓒ Timmy's soccer coach found a watch and returned it.

Ⓓ Two brothers learn to share.

Directions: Here is a story about a girl named Amy. Read the story to find out what she dreams about doing. Then answer questions 9–12.

> Amy had always dreamed of one day playing the trumpet. Well, it seemed that day had finally arrived. Amy's band teacher handed her a shiny new trumpet. Amy raised it to her lips and blew. Nothing happened. She blew harder. "BRAAGH!" What an awful noise!
>
> "Put your lips together and buzz," said Amy's teacher. Amy "buzzed" into the trumpet. She sounded like a sick fly. She tried again. This time the buzzing tickled her lips, and she laughed.
>
> "Keep trying," said her teacher. "Before you know it, you'll be making beautiful music."
>
> Just then a fly buzzed next to Amy's ear and woke her up.
>
> "Oh, my," she said. "I've been dreaming about my dream."

9. Which is the best title for this story?

  Ⓐ "Amy's Band Teacher"

  Ⓑ "Playing in the Band"

  Ⓒ "Amy's Dream"

  Ⓓ "Making Music"

10. Amy had always dreamed that someday she would

  Ⓐ join a band

  Ⓑ make an awful noise

  Ⓒ buzz like a fly

  Ⓓ play the trumpet

11. What made Amy laugh?

  Ⓐ A fly buzzed next to her ear.

  Ⓑ "Buzzing" into the trumpet tickled her lips.

  Ⓒ She had a funny dream.

  Ⓓ Her band teacher told her a joke.

12. Who handed Amy a shiny new trumpet?

  Ⓐ Amy's parents

  Ⓑ a student

  Ⓒ the store clerk

  Ⓓ the band teacher

Language Arts

PRACTICE 17 • Composition

SAMPLES

Directions: Read the paragraph. Then answer the questions that follow.

Mary Cassatt

She was famous for her drawings of children. Her favorite subjects to
   (1)   (2)
paint were mothers and children. The children, especially, liked to
                              (3)
pose for Cassatt because she always had candy, toys, and books for

them. Mary Cassatt worked for many years but was forced to stop
      (4)
painting later in life when she went blind. She died in 1926 at the age
                                                        (5)
of eighty-one.

A. Which sentence would best fit at the beginning of this paragraph before sentence 1?

Ⓐ In her day, most artists were men.

Ⓑ Mary Cassatt was an American painter born in 1845.

Ⓒ Mary Cassatt lived in France.

Ⓓ One of Cassatt's best friends was the French painter Edgar Degas.

B. The author probably wrote this passage to —

Ⓐ encourage girls to become artists

Ⓑ tell about a famous American painter

Ⓒ explain how artists work

Ⓓ describe women of the 1800s

Tips and Reminders

• The topic sentence should tell what the paragraph is about. Every sentence in that paragraph should support, or be about, that topic.

• To decide on the author's purpose in writing a passage, think about what the author is trying to say.

Go On →

PRACTICE

Directions: Read the paragraph. Then answer questions 1–4.

The Wolf and the Heron

It hurt the wolf to swallow. He had to find someone to take the bone
(1)   (2)
out of his throat. A short time later, the wolf met a heron with a long,
(3)
pointed beak. The wolf asked the heron to help him and offered to
(4)
give the heron a great present. When the heron agreed, the wolf
(5)
opened his mouth and the heron stuck her head inside. With her beak
(6)
she gently pulled out the bone. The wolf thanked the heron and
(7)
started to walk away.

---

1. The author probably wrote this story to –

  Ⓐ convince people to stay away from wolves

  Ⓑ tell an amusing story

  Ⓒ give information about herons

  Ⓓ show how wolves behave

2. Which sentence would best begin this paragraph?

  Ⓐ A wolf got a bone stuck in its throat.

  Ⓑ The wolf could not eat.

  Ⓒ Wolves and herons do not get along.

  Ⓓ The wolf had some presents.

3. Which sentence could be added to the paragraph after sentence 3?

  Ⓐ The wolf looked around.

  Ⓑ A heron has long thin legs.

  Ⓒ The wolf approached the heron.

  Ⓓ The wolf got the bone out himself.

4. Which sentence could be added at the end of the paragraph after sentence 7?

  Ⓐ The wolf felt sorry for the heron.

  Ⓑ "Hey," said the heron, "what about my present?"

  Ⓒ The wolf decided he would never trust a heron again.

  Ⓓ Disappointed, the heron left.

Directions: Read the paragraph. Then answer questions 5–8.

Sneakers

Back then, shoes had soles made of leather. Then people started using
 (1)   (2)
rubber to make soles. They found that the shoes were not only lighter,
                          (3)
but they were quieter. They started calling them "sneakers." In 1917,
            (4)   (5)
U.S. Rubber started making sneakers for kids. They called them "Keds."
                                                      (6)

Keds was a word that U.S. Rubber made up by putting together the
  (7)
words "kids" and "ped," which means "foot" in Latin. The Keds had
                                                      (8)

rubber soles and the tops were made of canvas.

---

5. Which would be the best topic sentence for this paragraph?

Ⓐ A company called Nike started making sneakers in the 1960s.

Ⓑ Sneakers have not changed for a long time.

Ⓒ Shoes have changed a lot since the early 1900s.

Ⓓ Sneakers are a lot like shoes, only quieter.

6. Which sentence could be added to the paragraph after sentence 3?

Ⓐ Today, almost everyone owns a pair of sneakers.

Ⓑ Work boots still have leather soles, though.

Ⓒ Sneakers come in all sizes and colors.

Ⓓ The shoes were so quiet, a person could sneak up on someone.

7. Which sentence could be added to the end of the paragraph after sentence 8?

Ⓐ Sneakers today are not made for kids.

Ⓑ Canvas is a strong, heavy cloth made of cotton.

Ⓒ Today's sneakers cost a lot of money.

Ⓓ Some sneakers today have waffle soles.

8. The author probably wrote this story to —

Ⓐ describe how shoes have changed over the years

Ⓑ explain how to make Keds

Ⓒ describe how easy it is to invent new things

Ⓓ convince people to buy Keds

Go On

Directions: Read the letter. Then answer questions 9–12.

Dear Aunt Claudia,

How did you know I needed a new baseball glove? I've been using my
 (1)   (2)
dad's glove from when he was a kid. It's so old it's starting to
                                           (3)
fall apart.

   I really love my new glove. It's the perfect size. I used it in my
     (4)   (5)   (6)
baseball game the other day, and I caught a pop fly! Maybe when you
                                                       (7)
visit next week, you can come watch our game on Saturday. Oh, and
                                                          (8)
don't forget to bring your glove so we can play catch. Thanks again!
                                                        (9)
                                         Love,

                                         Nicholas

---

9. Which sentence would best begin this letter?

   (A) Baseball is my favorite sport.

   (B) Are you still planning to come visit next week?

   (C) I have a baseball game on Saturday.

   (D) Thank you for the birthday present.

10. Which sentence could be added after sentence 3 in the first paragraph?

   (A) When I try to catch a ball with it, the ball falls out.

   (B) Did you and my dad ever play catch when you were kids?

   (C) Dad says baseball gloves cost a lot these days.

   (D) I wish it were my birthday every day.

11. Which sentence could be added at the end of this letter after sentence 9?

   (A) My team has only lost one game so far.

   (B) You're the best aunt a kid could ever have.

   (C) I also wanted a new bike for my birthday.

   (D) When baseball is over, I'll probably start soccer.

12. Nicholas wrote this letter to –

   (A) tell Aunt Claudia about baseball

   (B) ask Aunt Claudia to come visit

   (C) thank Aunt Claudia for a present

   (D) show Aunt Claudia that he's a good baseball player

PRACTICE 18 • Computation

Directions: Find the answer to each problem. If the answer is not given, choose N for "Not given."

SAMPLES

A. $5 + 8 =$
- Ⓐ 12
- Ⓑ 13
- Ⓒ 40
- Ⓓ N

B.
$$\begin{array}{r} 16 \\ -\ 4 \\ \hline \end{array}$$
- Ⓐ 13
- Ⓑ 17
- Ⓒ 20
- Ⓓ N

C. $6 \times 8 =$
- Ⓐ 14
- Ⓑ 48
- Ⓒ 54
- Ⓓ N

D. $63 \div 9 =$
- Ⓐ 7
- Ⓑ 54
- Ⓒ 567
- Ⓓ N

Tips and Reminders

- Look at the sign to see if you need to add (+), subtract (–), multiply (×), or divide (÷ or $\overline{)}$).

- Always check your answer.

- When you add or subtract numbers with decimals, make sure you line up the decimal points before adding or subtracting.

PRACTICE

1. $7 + 9 =$
- Ⓐ 12
- Ⓑ 16
- Ⓒ 63
- Ⓓ N

2.
$$\begin{array}{r} 24 \\ -\ 8 \\ \hline \end{array}$$
- Ⓐ 16
- Ⓑ 26
- Ⓒ 32
- Ⓓ N

3. 9×8

- (A) 17
- (B) 72
- (C) 81
- (D) N

9. $78 + 22$

- (A) 56
- (B) 90
- (C) 100
- (D) N

4. $28 \div 7 =$

- (A) 4
- (B) 5
- (C) 21
- (D) N

10. $36 \div 3 =$

- (A) 11
- (B) 12
- (C) 33
- (D) N

5. $37 + 5$

- (A) 32
- (B) 42
- (C) 87
- (D) N

11. $\$7.60 + \$2.47 =$

- (A) $7.84
- (B) $9.07
- (C) $10.07
- (D) N

6. $67 - 48$

- (A) 19
- (B) 21
- (C) 115
- (D) N

12. $24 + 6 + 194 =$

- (A) 224
- (B) 264
- (C) 494
- (D) N

7. $45 \div 9 =$

- (A) 6
- (B) 7
- (C) 54
- (D) N

13. $543 + 36$

- (A) 507
- (B) 549
- (C) 579
- (D) N

8. $\$1.24 - \$0.59 =$

- (A) $0.63
- (B) $0.73
- (C) $1.19
- (D) N

14. $252 - 7$

- (A) 152
- (B) 244
- (C) 259
- (D) N

15. $4 \times 72 =$
- (A) 288
- (B) 292
- (C) 298
- (D) N

16. $\$6.42 + \$2.54 =$
- (A) $3.88
- (B) $8.96
- (C) $9.16
- (D) N

17.
$$\begin{array}{r} 12 \\ 20 \\ + 57 \\ \hline \end{array}$$
- (A) 80
- (B) 89
- (C) 99
- (D) N

18. $204 - 105 =$
- (A) 99
- (B) 109
- (C) 309
- (D) N

19. $147 - 29 =$
- (A) 118
- (B) 122
- (C) 128
- (D) N

20. $7\overline{)56}$
- (A) 7
- (B) 8
- (C) 9
- (D) N

21. $400 \times 4 =$
- (A) 16
- (B) 160
- (C) 1600
- (D) N

22. $81 \div 9 =$
- (A) 8
- (B) 9
- (C) 90
- (D) N

23. $44 + 6 + 213 =$
- (A) 253
- (B) 263
- (C) 359
- (D) N

24.
$$\begin{array}{r} 584 \\ + 130 \\ \hline \end{array}$$
- (A) 454
- (B) 614
- (C) 714
- (D) N

25.
$$\begin{array}{r} 401 \\ \times 3 \\ \hline \end{array}$$
- (A) 123
- (B) 403
- (C) 703
- (D) N

26.
$$\begin{array}{r} \$12.21 \\ + 10.00 \\ \hline \end{array}$$
- (A) $2.21
- (B) $22.21
- (C) $120.21
- (D) N

Go On

27. $52 \times 3 =$

    Ⓐ 56
    Ⓑ 156
    Ⓒ 176
    Ⓓ N

33.
$$\begin{array}{r} 12 \\ 14 \\ +23 \\ \hline \end{array}$$

    Ⓐ 47
    Ⓑ 49
    Ⓒ 139
    Ⓓ N

28.
$$\begin{array}{r} 362 \\ -81 \\ \hline \end{array}$$

    Ⓐ 191
    Ⓑ 281
    Ⓒ 381
    Ⓓ N

34. $6 \times 30 =$

    Ⓐ 18
    Ⓑ 108
    Ⓒ 1800
    Ⓓ N

29. $43 \times 10 =$

    Ⓐ 53
    Ⓑ 403
    Ⓒ 430
    Ⓓ N

35.
$$\begin{array}{r} 54 \\ \times 5 \\ \hline \end{array}$$

    Ⓐ 59
    Ⓑ 250
    Ⓒ 270
    Ⓓ N

30. $\$5.00 - \$1.39 =$

    Ⓐ $3.71
    Ⓑ $4.61
    Ⓒ $6.39
    Ⓓ N

36.
$$\begin{array}{r} \$1.79 \\ -0.86 \\ \hline \end{array}$$

    Ⓐ $0.83
    Ⓑ $0.93
    Ⓒ $2.65
    Ⓓ N

31.
$$\begin{array}{r} 278 \\ +123 \\ \hline \end{array}$$

    Ⓐ 355
    Ⓑ 391
    Ⓒ 401
    Ⓓ N

37. $862 - 11 =$

    Ⓐ 741
    Ⓑ 851
    Ⓒ 873
    Ⓓ N

32. $64 \div 8 =$

    Ⓐ 6
    Ⓑ 7
    Ⓒ 12
    Ⓓ N

38.
$$\begin{array}{r} 244 \\ +160 \\ \hline \end{array}$$

    Ⓐ 180
    Ⓑ 304
    Ⓒ 404
    Ⓓ N

Stop

PRACTICE 19 • Text Structure

SAMPLES

Directions: Read the passage. Then answer the questions that follow.

Honeybees are very hard workers. Each bee helps make food for all the bees that live in the hive. First, the worker bees leave the hive because they need to find flowers. Next, they gather pollen and nectar from the flowers and fly back to the hive. The nectar is used to make honey for food.

The queen bee works hard, too, but her job is different. The queen bee's job is to lay eggs–and lots of them! Later, the eggs will hatch into more worker bees.

A. What happens first?

(A) Worker bees fly back to the hive.

(B) The bees use nectar to make honey.

(C) Worker bees leave the hive to find flowers.

(D) Worker bees gather pollen.

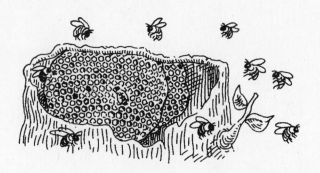

B. Why do worker bees leave the hive?

(A) They must find new homes.

(B) The hive is too crowded.

(C) They need to find flowers.

(D) The queen bee tells them to leave.

C. How is the queen bee different from the worker bees?

(A) She gathers pollen.

(B) She works very hard.

(C) She makes honey.

(D) She lays eggs.

Tips and Reminders

• Look for signal words in the passage.

To find the sequence of events, look for words such as *first, then, later, next.*

To find causes and effects, look for words such as *because, so, since, as a result.*

To compare things that are alike, look for words such as *like* or *same.* To contrast things that are different, look for words such as *unlike, but, on the other hand, different.*

Go On

PRACTICE

Directions: Read each passage and answer the questions that follow.

Kylee's Garden

Kylee wanted to grow her own vegetables, so she went to the store to get some seeds. She bought seeds for carrots, beans, beets, and lettuce.

When she got home, the first thing she did was till the soil in her garden. As soon as the soil was ready, Kylee planted the seeds and watered them.

After a few weeks, there were green plants everywhere. But they weren't carrots, beans, beets, and lettuce. Kylee's garden was filled with squashes, radishes, and eggplants!

1. Kylee bought some seeds because she wanted to

   Ⓐ feed them to the birds
   Ⓑ grow some flowers
   Ⓒ till the soil
   Ⓓ grow her own vegetables

2. What did Kylee do first when she got home?

   Ⓐ She tilled the soil.
   Ⓑ She bought some seeds.
   Ⓒ She planted the seeds.
   Ⓓ She watered the seeds.

3. What did Kylee do just after she planted the seeds?

   Ⓐ She tilled the soil.
   Ⓑ She watered the seeds.
   Ⓒ She picked some vegetables.
   Ⓓ She ate some carrots.

4. How was Kylee's garden different from what she expected?

   Ⓐ It was full of green plants.
   Ⓑ The plants were squashes, radishes, and eggplants.
   Ⓒ It was full of weeds.
   Ⓓ The plants did not grow.

How to Help a Bird Make a Nest

First, tie two or three pine cones together in a row. Next, cut several pieces of colored yarn. Drape a few pieces of yarn around each pine cone. Then go outside and tie the pine cones to a tree branch.

Like grass and small twigs, pieces of yarn make good nest-building material. But, the yarn is much more colorful. Birds will come and take the pieces of yarn because they can use them to make a nest.

5. What should you do first?

Ⓐ gather some grass and twigs

Ⓑ tie two or three pine cones together

Ⓒ cut several pieces of yarn

Ⓓ tie the pine cones to a tree branch

6. What should you do last?

Ⓐ tie the pine cones to a branch

Ⓑ put the yarn around the pine cones

Ⓒ find some colorful yarn

Ⓓ build a nest for the birds

7. Why will birds take the pieces of yarn?

Ⓐ The pieces of yarn look like worms.

Ⓑ The yarn will keep them warm.

Ⓒ They can use the yarn to build a nest.

Ⓓ They like to play with the yarn.

8. How is yarn different from grass and small twigs?

Ⓐ It can be cut in different lengths.

Ⓑ Yarn is more colorful.

Ⓒ It is good for building nests.

Ⓓ The birds will take it.

Dear Taylor,

We finally made it to Bell's Island yesterday. As soon as we arrived, I went for a swim in the ocean. Then Dad and I put up the tent. Later, we built a campfire and cooked hot dogs for dinner.

So far, I think this trip will be better than last year's. Already we've had one whole day without rain! There are fewer bugs this year, too.

I'll tell you more about everything when I get back next week.

Your friend,
Peter

9. How is Peter's trip different from last year's?

Ⓐ It's raining.

Ⓑ There aren't as many bugs.

Ⓒ The ocean is nearby.

Ⓓ Last year's trip was better.

10. What did Peter do first when he got to Bell's Island?

Ⓐ He helped his dad put up the tent.

Ⓑ He looked for bugs.

Ⓒ He went for a swim.

Ⓓ He ate dinner.

11. Peter and his dad built a campfire to

Ⓐ help them keep warm

Ⓑ give them light

Ⓒ scare the bugs away

Ⓓ cook dinner

Dinosaur Hunters

Dinosaurs lived millions of years ago, but the world has changed since then. Today, scientists cannot study live dinosaurs, so they hunt for dinosaur bones. The first thing dinosaur hunters must do is find a good place to look. Then they search for bones, which are often buried in rock. The dinosaur hunters use special tools to dig out the bones. They wrap the bones in plaster casts to protect them and then take them to a museum. At the museum, scientists study the bones to try to learn more about how dinosaurs lived.

12. Why do scientists wrap the bones in plaster casts?

Ⓐ to keep them safe

Ⓑ so people can study them

Ⓒ so the museum will take them

Ⓓ because they are broken

13. What do dinosaur hunters do first?

Ⓐ use special tools to dig out the bones

Ⓑ find a good place to look

Ⓒ take the bones to a museum

Ⓓ search for bones

14. How is the world of today different from the world as it was millions of years ago?

Ⓐ Today, there are no scientists.

Ⓑ The museums are all gone.

Ⓒ The world is much larger.

Ⓓ There are no living dinosaurs anymore.

PRACTICE 20 • Combining Sentences

Directions: Read the two sentences in the box. Choose the best way to combine them to form one sentence.

SAMPLE

> Darla rode her bicycle.
> She rode to Marcy's house.

Ⓐ Darla rode her bicycle, she rode to Marcy's house.

Ⓑ Darla rode her bicycle, so she rode to Marcy's house.

Ⓒ Darla rode her bicycle, and she rode to Marcy's house.

Ⓓ Darla rode her bicycle to Marcy's house.

Tips and Reminders

- Check the order of words in the combined sentence to make sure it is correct.

- Make sure the combined sentence has the same meaning as the two original sentences.

- Be careful in using conjunctions and connecting words, such as *and, but, so,* and *although.* Using an incorrect conjunction can change the meaning of the sentence.

PRACTICE

1. | Wesley loves to play soccer.
   | Wesley loves to play baseball.

   Ⓐ Wesley loves to play soccer and baseball.

   Ⓑ Wesley loves to play soccer, he loves to play baseball.

   Ⓒ Wesley loves to play soccer, but he loves to play baseball.

   Ⓓ Wesley loves to play soccer he also loves to play baseball.

2. | The pitcher threw the ball.
   | He threw it to first base.

   Ⓐ The pitcher threw the ball and threw it to first base.

   Ⓑ The pitcher threw the ball to first base.

   Ⓒ The pitcher threw the ball, he threw it to first base.

   Ⓓ The pitcher threw the ball he threw it to first base.

3. The boy ate his lunch early.
He was hungry.

(A) The boy ate his lunch early, he was hungry.

(B) The boy ate his lunch early he was hungry.

(C) The boy ate his lunch early because he was hungry.

(D) The boy ate his lunch early, so he was hungry.

4. The cat chased a mouse.
The cat caught the mouse.

(A) The cat chased a mouse, but caught it.

(B) The cat chased a mouse and caught it.

(C) The cat chased a mouse, the cat caught it.

(D) The cat chased a mouse the cat caught the mouse.

5. Mom cut the apple.
She cut it in half.

(A) Mom cut the apple, she cut it in half.

(B) Mom cut the apple because she cut it in half.

(C) Mom cut the apple she cut it in half.

(D) Mom cut the apple in half.

Directions: Read each paragraph. Then answer the questions.

Toby caught a turtle in the pond. It was a painted turtle. The turtle was sunning itself on a log and didn't see him approach. After Toby caught it, the turtle tried to bite him and get free. Toby felt sorry for the turtle. He threw it back into the pond.

6. How could the first two sentences best be combined?

(A) A painted turtle was caught by Toby in the pond.

(B) Toby caught a turtle in the pond, it was a painted turtle.

(C) Toby caught a turtle in the pond it was a painted turtle.

(D) Toby caught a painted turtle in the pond.

7. How could the last two sentences best be combined?

(A) Toby felt sorry for the turtle, so he threw it back into the pond.

(B) Toby felt sorry for the turtle because he threw it back into the pond.

(C) Toby felt sorry for the turtle, he threw it back into the pond.

(D) Toby felt sorry for the turtle, but he threw it back into the pond.

Porcupines have an excellent sense of smell. They also have good hearing. Their senses help to keep them safe. A porcupine's quills also help protect it. When a porcupine is attacked, it cannot shoot its quills as some people believe. The porcupine turns its back to the attacker. Its sharp quills stick into the attacker.

8. How could the first two sentences best be combined?

  (A) Porcupines have an excellent sense of smell, so they also have good hearing.

  (B) Porcupines have an excellent sense of smell and good hearing.

  (C) Porcupines have an excellent sense of smell they also have good hearing.

  (D) Porcupines have an excellent sense of smell, they also have good hearing.

9. How could the last two sentences best be combined?

  (A) The porcupine turns its back so its sharp quills stick into the attacker.

  (B) The porcupine turns its back to the attacker, its sharp quills stick into the attacker.

  (C) The porcupine turns its back to the attacker because its sharp quills stick into the attacker.

  (D) The porcupine turns its back to the attacker, but its sharp quills stick into the attacker.

Ezra ordered an ice-cream cone. He ordered it with sprinkles. The ice cream was melting fast, so Ezra ate quickly. He ate so fast he hardly tasted the ice cream. Ezra ordered another ice-cream cone. This time he ate it slowly.

10. How could the first two sentences best be combined?

  (A) Ezra ordered an ice-cream cone, he ordered it with sprinkles.

  (B) Ezra ordered an ice-cream cone he ordered it with sprinkles.

  (C) Ezra ordered an ice-cream cone with spinkles.

  (D) Ezra ordered an ice-cream cone, and he ordered it with sprinkles.

11. How could the last two sentences best be combined?

  (A) Ezra ordered another ice-cream cone, this time he ate it slowly.

  (B) Ezra ordered another ice-cream cone, but this time he ate it slowly.

  (C) Ezra ordered another ice-cream cone because this time he ate it slowly.

  (D) Ezra ordered another ice-cream cone this time he ate it slowly.

Stop

PRACTICE 21 • Estimation

SAMPLES

Directions: Choose the best answer to each question.

A. Keith paid $1.98 for a book and $0.97 for a pen. <u>About</u> how much did he spend in all?

   Ⓐ $2.00   Ⓒ $4.00

   Ⓑ $3.00   Ⓓ $5.00

B. Pia weighs 52 pounds. Toni weighs 69 pounds. Which numbers should you use to estimate how much more Toni weighs than Pia?

   Ⓐ 60 – 50

   Ⓑ 70 – 60

   Ⓒ 60 – 40

   Ⓓ 70 – 50

Tips and Reminders

- Underline or jot down important information to help you answer each question.

- Use rounding to estimate answers.

PRACTICE

1. Mr. Bates sold 68 roses, 41 daisies, and 39 petunias at his flower shop. <u>About</u> how many flowers did he sell in all?

   Ⓐ 100   Ⓒ 200

   Ⓑ 150   Ⓓ 250

2. Luanne buys a flag for $5.98. If she gives the clerk $10.00, <u>about</u> how much change should she receive?

   Ⓐ $6.00   Ⓒ $4.00

   Ⓑ $5.00   Ⓓ $3.00

3. Josie bought a baseball, a cap, and sunglasses. <u>About</u> how much did she spend altogether?

   Ⓐ $5   Ⓒ $15

   Ⓑ $10   Ⓓ $20

Go On

4. Kasha weighs 61 pounds, Juanita weighs 68 pounds, and Carlos weighs 72 pounds. <u>About</u> how many pounds do the children weigh altogether?

Ⓐ 100 lb   Ⓒ 200 lb
Ⓑ 150 lb   Ⓓ 250 lb

5. Kate bought some popcorn, a drink, and a fruit bar. <u>About</u> how much did she spend altogether?

Ⓐ $2   Ⓒ $6
Ⓑ $4   Ⓓ $10

6. Which numbers should you use to estimate 498 plus 305?

Ⓐ 500 + 300
Ⓑ 400 + 300
Ⓒ 500 + 400
Ⓓ 400 + 400

7. Sam bought 10 comic books at different prices. The least expensive one cost $4. The most expensive one cost $6. Which is the best estimate of how much money Sam spent for all of the comic books?

Ⓐ $30   Ⓒ $50
Ⓑ $40   Ⓓ $60

8. Third graders read 41 mysteries, 88 picture books, and 32 animal books. <u>About</u> how many books did they read altogether?

Ⓐ 140   Ⓒ 180
Ⓑ 160   Ⓓ 200

9. Jason had 412 stamps in his stamp collection. He bought 149 more stamps. Which numbers should you use to estimate how many stamps he had in all?

Ⓐ 400 + 150
Ⓑ 500 + 200
Ⓒ 400 + 200
Ⓓ 500 + 100

10. Alan bought new hockey pants for $89.49. He gave the clerk $100. <u>About</u> how much change should he receive?

Ⓐ $5   Ⓒ $15
Ⓑ $10   Ⓓ $20

11. A club sold boxes of cookies to raise money. <u>About</u> how many more boxes of peanut butter cookies were sold than boxes of ginger snaps?

79   23

Ⓐ 100   Ⓒ 60
Ⓑ 80   Ⓓ 20

12. Aaron sold 7 of his books at a garage sale. He sold each book for $2.99. <u>About</u> how much money did he receive for all his books?

   Ⓐ $7   Ⓒ $21

   Ⓑ $14   Ⓓ $28

13. The chart below shows how many pages Natasha read on different days. <u>About</u> how many pages did Natasha read altogether?

Day	Number of Pages
Monday	28
Tuesday	36
Thursday	18
Sunday	49

   Ⓐ 100   Ⓒ 120

   Ⓑ 110   Ⓓ 140

14. Suzie bought a marker, a pair of scissors, and a watercolor set. <u>About</u> how much did she spend in all?

   Ⓐ $7   Ⓒ $9

   Ⓑ $8   Ⓓ $11

15. Daryl bought 10 balloons for different prices. The least expensive balloon cost $1. The most expensive one cost $3. Which is the most reasonable estimate of how much money Daryl paid for all of the balloons?

   Ⓐ $10   Ⓒ $25

   Ⓑ $20   Ⓓ $30

16. Hamburgers cost $1.45 each at Joe's Diner. Which is the best estimate of the cost for 8 hamburgers?

   Ⓐ $0.12   Ⓒ $12.00

   Ⓑ $1.20   Ⓓ $120.00

17. Each section of the radio tower is 18 ft. Which is the best estimate of the height of the radio tower?

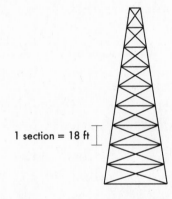

1 section = 18 ft

   Ⓐ 240 ft   Ⓒ 200 ft

   Ⓑ 220 ft   Ⓓ 180 ft

18. Farmer Davis had 224 cows. She bought 38 more cows. <u>About</u> how many cows did she have in all?

   Ⓐ 260   Ⓒ 220

   Ⓑ 240   Ⓓ 200

PRACTICE 22 • Inferences

Directions: Read each passage. Then answer the questions that follow.

SAMPLES

Tino blew his nose and wiped his eyes. "How could this have happened to me?" he asked himself as he looked in the mirror. "I just can't go to school looking like this!" Suddenly, Tino had an idea. He pulled a hat over his head and said to himself, "I'll wear this until it grows out."

A. What is bothering Tino?

  Ⓐ He doesn't like his haircut.

  Ⓑ He has nothing nice to wear.

  Ⓒ He is angry with his sister.

  Ⓓ He is feeling ill.

B. What will Tino probably do next?

  Ⓐ He will go back to bed.

  Ⓑ He will buy a wig.

  Ⓒ He will wear his hat to school.

  Ⓓ He will stay home from school.

Tips and Reminders

- To answer these kinds of questions, look for clues in the passage.

- Check each answer choice to decide which is most likely. Rule out any answers that are not supported by details in the passage.

PRACTICE

Something had awakened Shem, but he didn't know what it was. He lay there in the dark and listened. He saw a quick flash of light, and then it was dark again. He heard a soft, steady sound like pebbles against the window. A crashing sound made him jump. At last he realized what had awakened him, and he wasn't frightened anymore.

1. What had awakened Shem?

  Ⓐ someone tapping at the window

  Ⓑ a thunderstorm

  Ⓒ an airplane overhead

  Ⓓ a flashlight

Go On

Getting Our Feet Wet

Eight girls and five of us boys stood in a line waiting for Pam's brother, Joe. When the door opened and Joe walked through, everyone clapped and cheered.

Joe teaches people how to swim. This summer, Joe is giving free swimming lessons to all the kids in our town. He thinks that we should all know how to swim so we can feel safe around water. When Joe was our age, he fell out of a canoe and almost drowned. He wants to make sure that never happens to any of us.

"Okay," cried Joe as he walked toward us. "Everyone into the water!"

2. Where does this story take place?

   Ⓐ in a gym

   Ⓑ at a school

   Ⓒ in a lake

   Ⓓ at a swimming pool

3. What will probably happen next?

   Ⓐ Joe will give the kids a swimming lesson.

   Ⓑ The kids will refuse to go into the water.

   Ⓒ Joe will tell Pam to stay out of the water.

   Ⓓ The kids will cry because they are afraid of the water.

4. Joe is most likely giving the kids free swimming lessons because –

   Ⓐ he doesn't have a job

   Ⓑ he cares about them

   Ⓒ the kids' parents asked him to do it

   Ⓓ the kids asked him for lessons

5. What can you tell about Joe from reading this passage?

   Ⓐ He doesn't know how to swim.

   Ⓑ He is older than the kids.

   Ⓒ The kids don't like him.

   Ⓓ He wants to earn some money.

Frozen Banana Pops

To make frozen banana pops, you will need:

    1 cup orange juice
    3 bananas, cut in chunks
    2 tablespoons of sugar
    7 ($3\frac{1}{2}$ oz.) paper cups
    wooden sticks

Pour the orange juice into a blender. Add the bananas and sugar. Cover and mix until blended. Pour the mixture into the paper cups and place the cups in the freezer. Take the cups out when the mixture is partly frozen and put a wooden stick in each cup. Freeze until firm. To eat, peel off the paper cup. Makes 7.

WANTED Used hockey skates in good shape. Need size 5. Will pay up to $50 for good skates. Call me if you have what I'm looking for. 555-4329. Ask for Robbie.

FOR SALE Used hockey skates. Size 5. Only been used one season. Paid $130.00 new. Will sell for $55.00 or best offer. Call Wayne 555-7934.

---

6. The wooden stick in each cup will be used to –

  Ⓐ make the banana pop taste better

  Ⓑ stir in the banana chunks

  Ⓒ make the banana pop freeze faster

  Ⓓ hold the pop when you eat it

7. If you follow the directions exactly, how many wooden sticks will you need?

  Ⓐ 2

  Ⓑ 5

  Ⓒ 7

  Ⓓ 10

8. Where did these ads probably appear?

  Ⓐ a local newspaper

  Ⓑ a children's magazine

  Ⓒ a telephone book

  Ⓓ a school newsletter

9. What will Wayne most likely do if he sees Robbie's ad?

  Ⓐ give the skates to Robbie for free

  Ⓑ lower the price of the skates

  Ⓒ call Robbie

  Ⓓ wait for Robbie to phone him

10. What will Robbie probably do if he sees Wayne's ad?

  Ⓐ He will think that Wayne is a good hockey player.

  Ⓑ He will try to buy Wayne's skates for $50.00.

  Ⓒ He will ask Wayne to join his hockey team.

  Ⓓ He will tell Wayne that his price is much too high.

A Wild Ride

Jason stood beside his older sister, Meg, and stared at the river. The white water roared and bubbled as it rushed past them and crashed over the rocks. Both Jason and Meg wore bike helmets and life jackets, but Jason was not sure he wanted to get into the rubber raft.

"All right, we're ready," said the guide as he pulled the raft into the water. "Let's climb in."

Jason let his sister drag him into the raft, and he held onto the sides for dear life. The raft slowly drifted away from the shore until it reached the rushing water. As the raft shook and then shot down the river, Jason screamed. He held on tight as the raft bounced over the rocks and water sprayed everywhere. Jason got soaked in minutes, and his heart was racing.

Then suddenly, the raft charged around a bend and floated into calm, quiet water. The guide paddled the raft to the shore, and Jason climbed out.

"Wow! That was great!" he cried. "When does the next ride start?"

11. What will Jason probably do next?

   Ⓐ go home

   Ⓑ go swimming in the river

   Ⓒ go for another ride

   Ⓓ go hiking with Meg

12. How did Jason feel at first as he stood and stared at the river?

   Ⓐ scared

   Ⓑ angry

   Ⓒ hurt

   Ⓓ excited

13. You can tell from reading this passage that Jason –

   Ⓐ enjoyed the ride

   Ⓑ did not have a good time

   Ⓒ was glad the ride was over

   Ⓓ would never do this again

14. People who ride in rubber rafts have to wear helmets and life jackets to –

   Ⓐ keep warm

   Ⓑ be safe

   Ⓒ look sporty

   Ⓓ add weight to the raft

Language Arts

PRACTICE 23 • Revising

SAMPLES

Directions: Use this paragraph to answer the questions.

(1) The children in Katrin's class wrote their own play. (2) They retold a fairy tale in their own words and acted it out. (3) Katrin's favorite fairy tale is *Cinderella*. (4) Some children made the costumes. (5) Others wrote songs for the play. (6) Katrin's teacher said it was one of the best plays ever seen by her.

A. Which sentence should be left out of this paragraph?

- Ⓐ Sentence 2
- Ⓑ Sentence 3
- Ⓒ Sentence 4
- Ⓓ Sentence 5

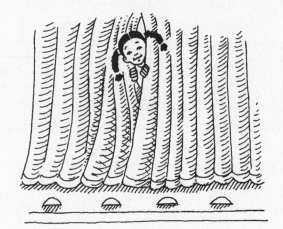

B. Which is the best way to rewrite the last sentence in this paragraph?

- Ⓐ It was one of the best plays ever was said by Katrin's teacher.
- Ⓑ It was one of the best plays ever seen by Katrin's teacher.
- Ⓒ Said by Katrin's teacher was one of the best plays ever seen by her.
- Ⓓ Katrin's teacher said it was one of the best plays she had ever seen.

Tips and Reminders

- To find a sentence that does not fit, decide what the paragraph is mostly about. Then look for the sentence that does not support the rest of the paragraph.

- To revise a sentence, choose the best way to rewrite it. Make sure the revised sentence has the same meaning as the original sentence.

Go On ➔

PRACTICE

Directions: Use this paragraph to answer questions 1–2.

(1) Gretchen spent the summer on her grandma's farm. (2) Her job was to help feed and water the animals. (3) She fed the ducks and the chickens, and sometimes she helped milk the cows. (4) Gretchen worked hard, but she had fun, too. (5) Gretchen doesn't own a horse. (6) Grandma's horses, everyday after her chores were done, she got to ride.

1. Which sentence should be left out of this paragraph?

   Ⓐ Sentence 2

   Ⓑ Sentence 3

   Ⓒ Sentence 4

   Ⓓ Sentence 5

2. Which is the best way to rewrite the last sentence in this paragraph?

   Ⓐ Grandma's horses she got to ride after her chores were done everyday.

   Ⓑ Everyday after her chores were done, she got to ride Grandma's horses.

   Ⓒ After her chores were done, she got to ride everyday Grandma's horses.

   Ⓓ Everyday her chores were done after she got to ride Grandma's horses.

Directions: Use this paragraph to answer questions 3–4.

(1) An elephant's trunk has many uses. (2) It can be used by the elephant for eating and drinking. (3) Elephants have only four teeth in their mouths. (4) Elephants can pick up food with their trunks and place it in their mouths. (5) An elephant can also use its trunk for bathing. (6) A shower can be given to itself by the elephant by spraying water from its trunk.

3. Which sentence should be left out of this paragraph?

   Ⓐ Sentence 2

   Ⓑ Sentence 3

   Ⓒ Sentence 4

   Ⓓ Sentence 5

4. Which is the best way to rewrite the last sentence in this paragraph?

   Ⓐ By spraying water from its trunk, a shower can be given to itself by an elephant.

   Ⓑ A shower by the elephant can be given to itself by spraying water from its trunk.

   Ⓒ An elephant can give itself a shower by spraying water from its trunk.

   Ⓓ A shower, an elephant can give itself, by spraying water from its trunk.

Directions: Use this paragraph to answer questions 5–6.

(1) Marina loves to go to the ocean. (2) She enjoys walking along the beach in her bare feet. (3) She spends hours swimming and collecting shells, and she takes the shells home with her. (4) Marina's sister loves the ocean, too. (5) Back home, when she looks at the shells, she remembers the ocean and Marina feels happy.

5. Which sentence should be left out of this paragraph?

Ⓐ Sentence 2

Ⓑ Sentence 3

Ⓒ Sentence 4

Ⓓ Sentence 5

6. Which is the best way to rewrite the last sentence in this paragraph?

Ⓐ She remembers the ocean and Marina feels happy back home when she looks at the shells.

Ⓑ When Marina looks at the shells, she remembers the ocean and feels happy back home.

Ⓒ When Marina looks at the shells, she remembers the ocean back home and feels happy.

Ⓓ Back home, when Marina looks at the shells, she remembers the ocean and feels happy.

Directions: Use this paragraph to answer questions 7–8.

(1) Mason got a new puppy last week, and it loves to chew things. (2) Already it has chewed one of Mason's shoes and his favorite shirt. (3) Yesterday, the puppy went into Mason's room and made a mess. (4) It took Mason two hours to clean it up. (5) Mason's friend Jake has a new puppy, too. (6) Owning a puppy is hard work, Mason is finding out.

7. Which sentence should be left out of this paragraph?

Ⓐ Sentence 2

Ⓑ Sentence 3

Ⓒ Sentence 4

Ⓓ Sentence 5

8. Which is the best way to rewrite the last sentence in this paragraph?

Ⓐ Mason is finding out that owning a puppy is hard work.

Ⓑ Hard work is owning a puppy, Mason is finding out.

Ⓒ Hard work is finding out Mason is owning a puppy.

Ⓓ Mason is finding out that hard work is owning a puppy.

Mathematics

PRACTICE 24 • Interpreting Data

SAMPLES

Directions: Natalie made this tally chart showing how many times she ate each kind of food during the week. Use the chart to answer the questions.

Kind of Food	Number of Times Eaten
Bread	＋＋＋ ＋＋＋ I
Fruit	＋＋＋ II
Milk/cheese	＋＋＋ ＋＋＋ III
Meat	III
Sweets	＋＋＋ III

A. How many times did Natalie eat fruit?

- Ⓐ 18
- Ⓑ 13
- Ⓒ 7
- Ⓓ 2

B. Which kind of food did she eat most often?

- Ⓐ Bread
- Ⓑ Fruit
- Ⓒ Milk/cheese
- Ⓓ Sweets

Tips and Reminders

- Study the graph or chart carefully. Use it to answer the questions.

- After choosing an answer, read the question again to make sure you have answered it correctly.

PRACTICE

Directions: Jack made a chart showing the numbers of different animals he saw in the park. Use the chart to answer questions 1–3.

Animals	Number Seen
Squirrels	12
Chipmunks	8
Toads	4
Foxes	1
Rabbits	2

1. How many chipmunks did Jack see?

- Ⓐ 12
- Ⓑ 8
- Ⓒ 4
- Ⓓ 2

2. What animal did Jack see least?

- Ⓐ Chipmunks
- Ⓑ Toads
- Ⓒ Foxes
- Ⓓ Rabbits

3. How many more squirrels than rabbits did Jack see?

- Ⓐ 10
- Ⓑ 8
- Ⓒ 6
- Ⓓ 4

Go On

Directions: Elise kept track of the number of miles she rode her bike each day. She put the results in a bar graph. Use the graph to answer questions 4–6.

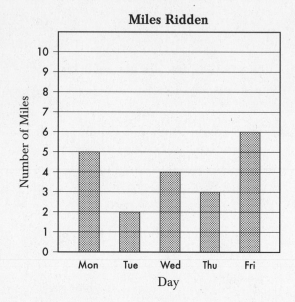

Miles Ridden

Directions: Dana made this table to show the number of plants sold at the plant sale. Use the table to answer questions 7–9.

Plant Sale

Type of Plant	Number Sold
Petunias	28
Daisies	19
Roses	14
Mums	26
Pansies	33

4. On which day did Elise ride exactly 3 miles?

  (A) Monday   (C) Wednesday

  (B) Tuesday   (D) Thursday

5. On which day did she ride 2 more miles than on Wednesday?

  (A) Monday   (C) Thursday

  (B) Tuesday   (D) Friday

6. How many miles did Elise ride on Monday and Tuesday together?

  (A) 7 miles   (C) 11 miles

  (B) 9 miles   (D) 13 miles

7. How many more pansies were sold than daisies?

  (A) 4   (C) 24

  (B) 14   (D) 52

8. Compared to roses, Dana sold exactly 2 times as many –

  (A) petunias   (C) mums

  (B) daisies   (D) pansies

9. How many petunias and mums together were sold?

  (A) 33   (C) 45

  (B) 40   (D) 54

Go On →

Directions: Leah's class voted on a class trip. They kept track of the number of votes for each choice and put the results in a bar graph. Use the graph to answer questions 10–13.

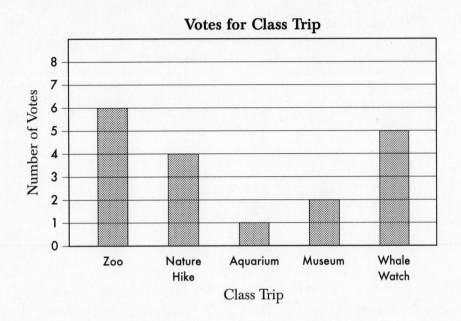

10. Which class trip got exactly 4 votes?

   Ⓐ Zoo
   Ⓑ Nature Hike
   Ⓒ Museum
   Ⓓ Whale Watch

11. Which class trip got exactly 3 more votes than the trip to the museum?

   Ⓐ Zoo
   Ⓑ Nature Hike
   Ⓒ Aquarium
   Ⓓ Whale Watch

12. Which class trip got the fewest votes?

   Ⓐ Nature Hike
   Ⓑ Museum
   Ⓒ Aquarium
   Ⓓ Whale Watch

13. How many students in all voted for the zoo and the whale watch?

   Ⓐ 12   Ⓒ 10
   Ⓑ 11   Ⓓ 9

Directions: Sarah asked her classmates to vote for the sport they liked best. She put the results in a tally chart. Use the chart to answer questions 14–16.

Favorite Sports

Sport	Number of Votes
Soccer	ﾐ ﾞ ﾞ
Baseball	ﾞ
Basketball	ﾞ
Tennis	ﾞ
Hockey	ﾞ

Directions: Evan made this chart to show the number of vegetables picked from his family garden. Use the chart to answer questions 17–18.

Vegetables Picked

Type of Vegetable	Number Picked
Beets	35
Broccoli	12
Carrots	23
Cucumbers	24
Tomatoes	40

14. Which sport had exactly 2 more votes than soccer?

   Ⓐ Baseball   Ⓒ Tennis

   Ⓑ Basketball   Ⓓ Hockey

15. How many more students voted for baseball than tennis?

   Ⓐ 6   Ⓒ 4

   Ⓑ 5   Ⓓ 3

16. How many students in all voted for soccer, tennis, and hockey?

   Ⓐ 47   Ⓒ 38

   Ⓑ 41   Ⓓ 25

17. Evan picked 12 heads of broccoli and exactly twice as many –

   Ⓐ Beets

   Ⓑ Carrots

   Ⓒ Cucumbers

   Ⓓ Tomatoes

18. How many more tomatoes than carrots did Evan pick?

   Ⓐ 15   Ⓒ 21

   Ⓑ 17   Ⓓ 23

PRACTICE 25 • Story Elements

Directions: Read each passage. Then answer the questions that follow.

SAMPLES

Becky came home from school all excited. "We're going to have a jump rope club," she told her mother. "We're going to perform and raise money for children who are in the hospital."

"But you don't know how to jump rope," her mother said.

"I can learn!" Becky replied. And she did. She found a piece of rope and started jumping. Every time she missed, she simply started again. In just a few days, she was ready to join the club.

A. Which word best describes Becky?

- Ⓐ hard-working
- Ⓑ lazy
- Ⓒ bored
- Ⓓ honest

B. What lesson can be learned from this story?

- Ⓐ Not everyone is good at everything.
- Ⓑ You should keep the promises you make.
- Ⓒ You can do anything you put your mind to.
- Ⓓ Don't count your chickens before they hatch.

Tips and Reminders

- Look back at the passage to answer questions about details.
- For other questions, you may need to "read between the lines." Think about the story and what you already know to answer these questions.

PRACTICE

Paco went to visit his grandmother one spring day. The lot next to her apartment was filled with beautiful white daisies. There must have been hundreds and hundreds of them! Paco asked Nana where the flowers had come from.

"Magic," she said with a wink. "Let me give you a little magic to spread around." She handed Paco a dead flower. Its petals were dry and wrinkled. "This daisy is filled with seeds for another hundred. Each of them will make a hundred more."

Paco laughed to himself. "Magic, ha!" he thought. Even so, he stopped in a field near home and dropped the seeds in the dirt.

Years passed. Paco moved to a new town and grew up. One day he came back to visit his old home. As he walked by the field, he could not believe his eyes. Thousands of daisies bloomed where there once had been piles of trash. Magic, indeed!

1. Where does the beginning of the story take place?

Ⓐ at Nana's apartment

Ⓑ in a flower shop

Ⓒ in a field near Paco's home

Ⓓ in a town far away

2. What kind of story is this?

Ⓐ a story about animals that teaches a lesson

Ⓑ a story about something in space

Ⓒ a story about people who could be real

Ⓓ a story from a newspaper

3. Which of these best describes the mood of this story?

Ⓐ scary

Ⓑ sad

Ⓒ funny

Ⓓ hopeful

4. How did the flowers bloom in Paco's field?

Ⓐ They grew by magic.

Ⓑ They grew from the seeds Paco planted.

Ⓒ Paco's grandmother planted them.

Ⓓ They grew out of the trash.

Angie slowly carried her lunch tray into the cafeteria. She looked around the huge room for a face she knew. Angie waited for a voice to call her name, asking her to sit down. But no one noticed the new third grader.

Angie blinked quickly, afraid someone would see a tear slide down her check. She sat down at an empty table facing the wall. Lunch will last forever today, she thought. Next she would have no one to play with at recess.

Just then someone tapped Angie on the shoulder. "Don't sit here by yourself. Come join us over there," said Cassie, a girl in her class. "I saved you a place."

Angie grinned up at her new friend and picked up her lunch tray.

5. How does Angie feel at the beginning of the story?

   Ⓐ happy

   Ⓑ lonely

   Ⓒ angry

   Ⓓ sleepy

6. Where does this story take place?

   Ⓐ on the playground

   Ⓑ in a classroom

   Ⓒ in a restaurant

   Ⓓ in a lunchroom

7. What kind of story is this?

   Ⓐ a news story

   Ⓑ a fairy tale

   Ⓒ a story that could really happen

   Ⓓ a magazine article

8. What lesson can you learn from this story?

   Ⓐ It can be hard to move to a new place.

   Ⓑ It's easy to make new friends.

   Ⓒ It's fun to eat in new places.

   Ⓓ It's boring to play alone at recess.

Ricky's dad was a park ranger. In his free time, he went on rescue calls to save whales, seals, and other sea animals. One day Ricky and his dad were at the beach when Dad's beeper went off. He ran to a phone and came right back. "Let's go, son," he said. "There's a finback whale in trouble. It's tangled up in some fishing gear."

The two drove quickly to meet the rescue boat. "I guess you'll need to come along, Ricky," said his father.

Within minutes they spotted the whale from the boat. Dad jumped into the water wearing his wet suit. As other workers helped cut the lines and nets, Dad patted the whale's head. All the while he talked to it gently.

The whale seemed to know that everyone wanted to help. Instead of fighting and splashing, it held very still. When it was freed, the whale turned as if to say thanks. Then it flipped its huge tail and swam away.

"That's what I like," said Dad as he climbed back onto the boat. "Another happy ending."

9. Where does the rescue take place?

Ⓐ at sea

Ⓑ in a park

Ⓒ at the beach

Ⓓ on a fishing trip

10. Which of these best describes Ricky's dad?

Ⓐ lazy and careless

Ⓑ foolish but caring

Ⓒ brave but gentle

Ⓓ bored but helpful

11. Why did the workers cut the lines?

Ⓐ to untangle the whale

Ⓑ to stop people from fishing

Ⓒ to keep the whale from moving

Ⓓ to free the boat

12. What did the whale do at the end?

Ⓐ It splashed the workers with its tail to show that it was upset.

Ⓑ It turned toward the workers as if to say thanks.

Ⓒ It pushed Ricky's dad back to the boat.

Ⓓ It took all the lines and nets as it swam away.

Two friends were walking along a road together when one of them found a purse full of gold. "How lucky I am!" cried Nathan. He danced a little jig on the road and laughed.

"Do not say 'How lucky *I* am,' " said his friend Daniel. "Say 'How lucky *we* are,' for friends should share with each other."

"Oh, no," replied Nathan stubbornly. "I found it and so it's mine. I shall buy a new house with this gold, and I might buy some cows, too."

Just then they heard loud shouts of "Stop, thief!" Looking around, they saw an angry crowd of people coming toward them. Some of the men carried rakes, and one woman held a rolling pin in her hand.

Nathan grew frightened. "We will be in deep trouble if they find us with this purse!" he cried.

"What do you mean, '*We* will be in trouble'?" said Daniel. "You said the gold was yours. Therefore *you* are in trouble."

As a man from the crowd grabbed Nathan by the arm, Daniel turned and walked away.

13. What kind of story is this?

Ⓐ a news story

Ⓑ a make-believe story

Ⓒ a myth

Ⓓ a magazine article

14. The people in the crowd were angry because they thought that –

Ⓐ Daniel was running away

Ⓑ Nathan had taken their cows

Ⓒ Daniel and Nathan were fighting

Ⓓ Nathan had stolen the gold

15. What kind of person is Nathan?

Ⓐ selfish

Ⓑ brave

Ⓒ generous

Ⓓ silly

16. What is the theme of this story?

Ⓐ Good luck is usually followed by bad luck.

Ⓑ It is important to speak correctly at all times.

Ⓒ If you will not share your good luck, no one will help you in times of bad luck.

Ⓓ It is a good idea to hide valuable things so that others won't see them.

PRACTICE 26 • Locating Information

Directions: Choose the best answer to each question.

SAMPLES

Kim is writing a report on the elections that just took place in her town.

A. To find information for her story, Kim should look in –

  Ⓐ a magazine

  Ⓑ an encyclopedia

  Ⓒ a dictionary

  Ⓓ a newspaper

B. Kim wants to list the names of the winners of the election in alphabetical order. Which name should be listed first?

  Ⓐ Cleary

  Ⓑ Clark

  Ⓒ Clugman

  Ⓓ Clifton

Tips and Reminders

- Read carefully to figure out what kind of information is needed. Then decide which reference source has that kind of information.

- To put words in alphabetical order, look at the first letter of each word. If the first letters are the same, look at the second or third letters.

PRACTICE

Troy is making a model of a Native American longhouse. He is also writing a report on the people who lived in longhouses.

1. To find a picture of a longhouse, Troy should look in –

  Ⓐ a dictionary

  Ⓑ a newspaper

  Ⓒ an atlas

  Ⓓ a social studies book

2. To find information for his report, Troy should look in –

  Ⓐ a magazine

  Ⓑ an encyclopedia

  Ⓒ a dictionary

  Ⓓ a mathematics book

Rona is writing a report about exploring Mars.

3. Where could Rona find the most information about Mars?

Ⓐ a dictionary

Ⓑ a math book

Ⓒ a newspaper

Ⓓ an encyclopedia

4. Rona wants to learn about something that happened on Mars yesterday. Where should she look?

Ⓐ a newspaper

Ⓑ a science book

Ⓒ a dictionary

Ⓓ an encyclopedia

5. If Rona wanted to learn more about how to organize her report, she could check –

Ⓐ a dictionary

Ⓑ an atlas

Ⓒ an encyclopedia

Ⓓ a language arts book

6. Rona made a list of words to use in her report. She wanted to put them in alphabetical order to check them in the dictionary. Which word should be listed first?

Ⓐ rotate

Ⓑ receive

Ⓒ robot

Ⓓ research

7. Rona also listed these words to check in the dictionary. Which list is in correct alphabetical order?

Ⓐ Pluto - planet - plot - ply

Ⓑ planet - plot - Pluto - ply

Ⓒ plot - ply - planet - Pluto

Ⓓ ply - Pluto - plot- planet

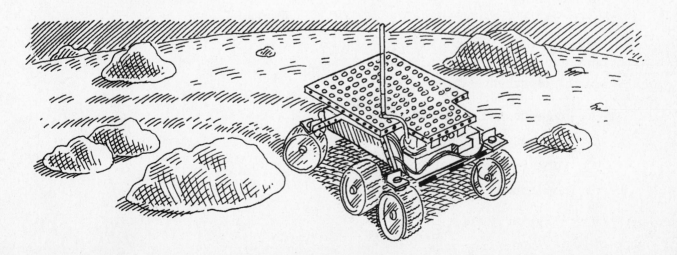

Marshall wants to make a map to show some important places in his state. He also plans to write a report to go with his map.

Tammy is writing a report about the lives of the colonists who first settled in Virginia. She wants to include drawings of colonial clothing.

8. Where could Marshall find a map to use for his work?

   (A) a social studies book

   (B) a newspaper

   (C) a magazine

   (D) a dictionary

9. Where could Marshall find information to use in his report?

   (A) a dictionary

   (B) an encyclopedia

   (C) a magazine

   (D) a newspaper

10. Marshall wanted to list the places on the map in alphabetical order. Which name should come first?

   (A) Alamo

   (B) Almira

   (C) Amarillo

   (D) Aleppo

11. Marshall wants to check some words in the dictionary. Which list is in correct alphabetical order?

   (A) neighbor - native - naval - newt

   (B) neighbor - newt - native - naval

   (C) native - naval - neighbor - newt

   (D) naval - native - neighbor - newt

12. To find information on how to make an outline for her report, Tammy should look in –

   (A) a magazine

   (B) an encyclopedia

   (C) a language arts book

   (D) a dictionary

13. To find pictures of colonial clothing, Tammy should look in –

   (A) a dictionary

   (B) a magazine

   (C) a newspaper

   (D) an encyclopedia

14. Tammy wants to list some important names in alphabetical order. Which name should come first?

   (A) Dare

   (B) Dawson

   (C) Davis

   (D) Dabney

PRACTICE 27 • Solving Problems

Directions: Choose the best answer to each question.

SAMPLES

A. Lucy bought 5 cat stickers. She gave away 2 stickers. Which question could you answer using this information?

    Ⓐ How much did Lucy pay for the stickers?

    Ⓑ How much change did Lucy get?

    Ⓒ How many stickers fit in Lucy's sticker book?

    Ⓓ How many stickers did Lucy have left?

B. Six scouts went camping. Each scout ate 2 hot dogs. Which number sentence should you use to find how many hot dogs they ate in all?

    Ⓐ $6 - 2 = \square$

    Ⓑ $2 \times 6 = \square$

    Ⓒ $6 + 2 = \square$

    Ⓓ $6 \div 2 = \square$

Tips and Reminders

- Underline or jot down important information to help you answer each question.

- Check each answer choice. Find the one that has all the information you need.

- Draw a picture if it helps you answer the question.

PRACTICE

1. Kathy asks 3 friends to sleep over. Each friend brings 2 games to play. Which number sentence should you use to find how many games they bring altogether?

    Ⓐ $2 + 3 = \square$

    Ⓑ $2 + 2 = \square$

    Ⓒ $3 \times 3 = \square$

    Ⓓ $2 \times 3 = \square$

2. Blair rode 2 miles on his bike to the store. Then he rode 3 more miles to the lake. Which question could you answer using this information?

    Ⓐ How much did he spend at the store?

    Ⓑ How long did he spend at the lake?

    Ⓒ How far is it to school?

    Ⓓ How many miles did he ride his bike in all?

3. Tory planted 3 rows of tomato plants. There were 4 plants in each row. Which number sentence should you use to find the number of plants in all?

   Ⓐ $4 \times 3 = \square$

   Ⓑ $4 + 3 = \square$

   Ⓒ $4 - 3 = \square$

   Ⓓ $4 + 4 = \square$

4. There are 3 shelves of books. Each shelf has 11 books. Which number sentence shows how to find the total number of books?

   Ⓐ $3 \times 11 = \square$

   Ⓑ $3 + 11 = \square$

   Ⓒ $3 \times 3 = \square$

   Ⓓ $11 + 11 = \square$

5. Sachi had 9 pencils. She gave 2 to April. Which question could you answer using this information?

   Ⓐ How many pencils did April use?

   Ⓑ What color were the pencils?

   Ⓒ How many pencils did Sachi have left?

   Ⓓ How long were the pencils?

6. There are 7 parking spaces in front of the store. There are cars in 3 of the spaces. Which question could you answer using this information?

   Ⓐ What color are the cars?

   Ⓑ How many spaces are empty?

   Ⓒ What kind of store is it?

   Ⓓ How long have the cars been parked?

7. There are 8 swings at the playground. Children are using 5 swings. Which question could you answer using this information?

   Ⓐ How many swings are empty?

   Ⓑ How old are the children?

   Ⓒ How many children are on the slide?

   Ⓓ What time does the playground close?

8. There are 5 boxes of pencils on a shelf. Each box has 8 pencils. Which number sentence should you use to find the total number of pencils?

   Ⓐ $5 + 8 = \square$

   Ⓑ $8 \div 5 = \square$

   Ⓒ $8 - 5 = \square$

   Ⓓ $5 \times 8 = \square$

9. Sarah earned 14 badges in scouts. Dolly earned 7 badges. Which number sentence shows how many more badges Sarah earned?

   Ⓐ $14 + 7 = \square$

   Ⓑ $14 - 7 = \square$

   Ⓒ $14 \div 7 = \square$

   Ⓓ $\square - 7 = 14$

10. May bought a book for $6.95. What information do you need to find how much change she should receive?

    Ⓐ the name of the book

    Ⓑ how many pages the book has

    Ⓒ where May bought the book

    Ⓓ how much money she gave the clerk

11. Barry lost 6 top teeth and 4 bottom teeth. Which question could you answer using this information?

ⒶHow many teeth are filled?

ⒷHow often does he brush his teeth?

ⒸHow many teeth did he lose in all?

ⒹDoes he wear braces on his teeth?

12.

Wanda had 32 marbles in 3 bags. She lost one of the bags. What information do you need to find how many marbles she had left?

Ⓐwhat kind of marbles she had

Ⓑwhy she put the marbles in 3 different bags

Ⓒwhere she lost the marbles

Ⓓhow many marbles were in each bag

13. Jerome scored 12 points in the first half of a basketball game. He scored 9 points in the second half. Which number sentence should you use to find how many points he scored in all?

Ⓐ $12 + 9 = \square$

Ⓑ $12 - 9 = \square$

Ⓒ $12 \div 9 = \square$

Ⓓ $12 + 2 = \square$

14.

Julie caught 14 fish. Al caught 7 fish. Which number sentence shows how to find how many fish they caught altogether?

Ⓐ $14 - 7 = \square$

Ⓑ $7 + \square = 14$

Ⓒ $7 + 14 = \square$

Ⓓ $14 \times 7 = \square$

15. Two friends shared equally a pack of 12 baseball cards. Which number sentence shows how to find the number of cards each one got?

Ⓐ $12 + 2 = \square$

Ⓑ $12 \div 2 = \square$

Ⓒ $2 \times 12 = \square$

Ⓓ $12 - 2 = \square$

16. On Saturday Chris bowled a score of 64 in his first game and 98 in his second game. Which question could you answer using this information?

ⒶWhat was Chris's score in the third game?

ⒷHow many times did Chris bowl in all on Saturday?

ⒸHow many points did Chris score on Friday?

ⒹHow many more points did Chris score in the second game than in the first game?

Go On

17. At 7:00 o'clock, Jen's family began to watch the first of 2 videos. The first one lasted 105 minutes. The second video was not as long. What information do you need to find what time the second video ended?

Ⓐ the names of the videos

Ⓑ how long the second video lasted

Ⓒ how much it cost to rent the two videos

Ⓓ the number of people in Jen's family

18. Amy took a 40-minute train ride. Then she took a 32-minute ride on a ferry. Which question could you answer using this information?

Ⓐ How long did she travel altogether?

Ⓑ How much more did the ferry cost than the train?

Ⓒ How many miles did she travel?

Ⓓ How long did she wait for the ferry?

19. Lauren had 16 beanbag animals. She got 4 more for her birthday. Which number sentence shows how to find the number of beanbag animals Lauren has in all?

Ⓐ $16 - 4 = \square$

Ⓑ $16 \div 4 = \square$

Ⓒ $16 \times 4 = \square$

Ⓓ $16 + 4 = \square$

20. Ms. Chen's class read 47 books for a reading contest. Mr. Rivera's class read 38 books. Which number sentence shows how to find how many more books Ms. Chen's class read?

Ⓐ $47 + 38 = \square$

Ⓑ $47 - 38 = \square$

Ⓒ $47 \times 38 = \square$

Ⓓ $47 \div 38 = \square$

21. A painter used 14 gallons of paint to paint the rooms on the first floor of a house. He used 12 gallons of paint on the second floor. What information do you need to find how many gallons he used in each room?

Ⓐ the number of rooms on each floor

Ⓑ the color of the paint

Ⓒ how fast the painter worked

Ⓓ when the painter finished

22. Melanie colored 64 eggs. She put an equal number of eggs in each of 8 baskets. Which number sentence should you use to find how many eggs she put in each basket?

Ⓐ $64 + 8 = \square$

Ⓑ $64 - 8 = \square$

Ⓒ $64 \times 8 = \square$

Ⓓ $64 \div 8 = \square$

Stop

PRACTICE 28 • Making Judgments

Directions: Read each passage. Then answer the questions that follow.

SAMPLES

Where's Mom?

Jackson's mom had the flu. She was sneezing and coughing as she lay in bed with a box of tissues.

Jackson was hungry, but he didn't want to bother Mom. He found a can of soup and warmed it up. Then he made two cheese sandwiches. He placed a bowl of soup and one of the sandwiches on a tray. As a final touch, he plucked a flower from a plant in the living room and put it in a cup next to the bowl.

Before he ate his dinner, Jackson carried the tray into his mother's room. "Oh, Jackson," Mom said when she saw him, "you're my hero!"

A. Which sentence states an opinion?

Ⓐ Jackson was hungry.

Ⓑ "You're my hero!"

Ⓒ Jackson's mom had the flu.

Ⓓ Then he made two cheese sandwiches.

B. Jackson probably thought that –

Ⓐ he was too young to cook

Ⓑ his mother was too sick to make dinner

Ⓒ his mother should be cooking dinner for him

Ⓓ his mother would sneeze when she smelled the flower

Tips and Reminders

• A fact is a statement that can be proven. An opinion is a belief or feeling that may or may not be true.

• As you read a passage, think about what the author is trying to say or why the author wrote the passage.

• To make a judgment or decision, think about the information in the passage. Look at all the answer choices and choose the most likely or most important one.

Go On

PRACTICE

What Happened to Sam?

Sam was a terrible bully. He liked to pick on smaller kids. He stepped on every bug he could find. He tied tin cans to the dog's tail, then laughed as the dog tried to shake off the cans.

One morning as Sam brushed his teeth, he looked in the mirror. He could not believe what he saw. Instead of eyes, giant feelers grew from his head. Shiny claws had replaced his arms. He looked like a large bug!

After breakfast Sam crawled outside, since he could no longer walk standing up. "Here I come," yelled a voice. A giant boy on a bike headed straight for Sam. "I'm small and helpless," Sam thought. "What can I do to save myself?"

Sam jumped out of the way and landed in a puddle. He could see his face reflected in the puddle and found that he had turned back into a boy. But Sam had learned an important lesson. He decided he would change his ways.

1. Which part of the story could **not** really happen?

   Ⓐ Sam looked in the mirror.

   Ⓑ A boy rode a bike toward Sam.

   Ⓒ Sam turned into a bug.

   Ⓓ A boy decided to change his ways.

2. What lesson did Sam learn?

   Ⓐ to feed his dog on time

   Ⓑ to ride a bike more safely

   Ⓒ to brush his teeth every day

   Ⓓ to be kind to other living things

3. The author probably wrote this story to –

   Ⓐ teach readers a lesson about kindness

   Ⓑ explain why it's no fun to be a bully

   Ⓒ describe how bugs are different from people

   Ⓓ make readers laugh at a boy turning into a bug

4. Which sentence states an opinion?

   Ⓐ He stepped on every bug he could find.

   Ⓑ Sam was a terrible bully.

   Ⓒ He looked in the mirror.

   Ⓓ Sam jumped out of the way and landed in a puddle.

Go On

Where Can the Dogs Play?

To the Editor:

I am writing to complain about a new law. I take my dog for a walk in the park every day after school. I let him run in the meadow with other dogs. He likes to catch sticks and balls that I throw. He's very well behaved, and he comes to me as soon as I call him. Since we live in an apartment, it's the only place he can get fresh air and exercise.

Yesterday, I took Sparky to the park as usual. There was a new sign that said "No Dogs Allowed." A police officer was there. She was telling people that she will start giving out tickets next week if their dogs are not leashed.

Who made this silly law? It's unfair to dog owners. It's really unfair to dogs! Let's get it changed right away.

George Clemente

5. The person who wrote this letter is probably a –

   Ⓐ dog hater
   Ⓑ police officer
   Ⓒ newspaper editor
   Ⓓ student

6. The author wrote this letter to –

   Ⓐ get a new law changed
   Ⓑ complain about dogs running loose in the park
   Ⓒ explain his dog's name
   Ⓓ keep dogs out of the park

7. Which statement is a fact?

   Ⓐ This law is unfair.
   Ⓑ My dog is very well behaved.
   Ⓒ This new law is silly.
   Ⓓ A police officer was in the park.

8. The author of this letter would probably agree that –

   Ⓐ every new law is a good one
   Ⓑ people should have a say about new laws before they are made
   Ⓒ people should not have pets
   Ⓓ people should not be allowed to walk on the grass in parks

Who Stole Bear's Honey?

Bear was angry. For several mornings he had gone to the cupboard for a pawful of honey. Each time he had found the honey jar empty.

"Those ants!" he yelled. "They've been in my honey again." The ants scurried from the room, too timid to tell Bear that they had not touched his honey.

Bear got more honey, but the next day it was gone again. "That bird!" he yelled. "She has stolen my honey." But Bird flew around Bear's head and told him she was innocent.

The next day the honey was gone again. "You bad Cat," Bear yelled. "Where's my honey?"

"Don't be silly," said Cat. "I hate to be sticky. I wouldn't touch your honey."

Before bed that night, Bear made a plan to catch the thief. He filled the pot of honey and placed it in the cupboard. He left the cupboard door open just a crack. At the top of the door he placed a jug of water, leaning against the cupboard. Whoever tried to open the cupboard would get a real surprise!

Bear went to bed, smiling about his plan. He couldn't wait to dream his favorite dream. In it he would lick sweet honey from a jar that never ran out. But Bear never got to that part of his dream. Instead he found himself wide awake. He was standing by the cupboard in a pool of water. He was soaking wet!

Bird, Cat, and the ants all had a good laugh that night. Bear never blamed anyone for stealing his honey again.

9. What happened in the story that could **not** happen in real life?

   Ⓐ A bird flew around a room.

   Ⓑ An animal took some honey.

   Ⓒ A bear made a secret plan.

   Ⓓ Ants scurried from a room.

10. What did Bear do that was unfair?

   Ⓐ He stored honey in his cupboard.

   Ⓑ He ate too much before he went to sleep.

   Ⓒ He accused others of stealing before he knew all the facts.

   Ⓓ He dreamed about eating honey.

11. Who really took Bear's honey during the night?

   Ⓐ the ants

   Ⓑ Bird

   Ⓒ Bear

   Ⓓ Cat

12. The author probably wrote this story to –

   Ⓐ describe how bears live

   Ⓑ teach readers a lesson

   Ⓒ compare bears with ants

   Ⓓ explain how honey is made

PRACTICE 29 • Reference Materials

SAMPLES

Directions: Use the title page to answer question A.

Directions: Use this part of a dictionary page to answer question B.

Alone at Sea

by Martin Guzzle

Published by Sandy Neck Press
Seaside, California

Dd

deceive
To trick someone

decent
Good or proper

defect
A fault or weakness

descend
To climb down to a lower level

A. This book was written by –

- Ⓐ Martin Guzzle
- Ⓑ Alone at Sea
- Ⓒ Sandy Neck
- Ⓓ Seaside

B. Which word best describes what you do when you walk downstairs?

- Ⓐ deceive
- Ⓑ decent
- Ⓒ defect
- Ⓓ descend

Tips and Reminders

- A title page gives the title of a book, the name of the author, and the name of the publisher. It also tells where the book was published.

- Use a table of contents to find out what is in each chapter. Use an index to find information on a certain topic.

- In a dictionary, guide words show the first and last entries on a dictionary page. All words on that page are listed in alphabetic order. Read the entries to check word meanings.

PRACTICE

Directions: Use the table of contents to answer questions 1–4.

A Handbook of Healthful Eating

Contents

1. In which chapter could you find out if beans have as much protein as meat?

Ⓐ Chapter 1

Ⓑ Chapter 3

Ⓒ Chapter 4

Ⓓ Chapter 5

2. Which of these would Chapter 1 probably explain?

Ⓐ how to prepare foods that don't cost a lot

Ⓑ why you should eat many different foods

Ⓒ how much fat is in a baked potato

Ⓓ how to make a low-fat main dish

3. In which chapter would you probably find a recipe for low-fat pies?

Ⓐ Chapter 1

Ⓑ Chapter 2

Ⓒ Chapter 5

Ⓓ Chapter 6

4. On what page should you begin reading to find ideas on eating fewer desserts?

Ⓐ page 3

Ⓑ page 29

Ⓒ page 46

Ⓓ page 94

Directions: Use the table of contents and the index to answer questions 5–6.

Taking Care of Your New Puppy

Index

5. Which chapter has information on how to make your puppy behave?

Ⓐ Chapter 1
Ⓑ Chapter 2
Ⓒ Chapter 3
Ⓓ Chapter 4

6. Which page probably tells what shots your puppy needs?

Ⓐ page 3
Ⓑ page 13
Ⓒ page 14
Ⓓ page 36

Directions: For each question, look at the guide words from a dictionary page. Choose the word that would be found on the same page of the dictionary.

7. | piano – pickax |

Ⓐ pitch
Ⓑ planet
Ⓒ phase
Ⓓ pick

8. | ocean – odor |

Ⓐ octopus
Ⓑ oak
Ⓒ origin
Ⓓ orbit

9. | side – signal |

Ⓐ shriek
Ⓑ shower
Ⓒ sight
Ⓓ silver

10. | lair – language |

Ⓐ ladybug
Ⓑ landfill
Ⓒ lend
Ⓓ life

11. | below – betray |

Ⓐ best
Ⓑ bedtime
Ⓒ believe
Ⓓ billion

Directions: Use the dictionary page to answer questions 12–16.

Gg

glider
Aircraft that flies on air currents instead of by an engine

goatee
Beard grown around the mouth and chin

gondola
A small boat with high pointed ends

guava
A tropical fruit used in jelly

guilty
Feeling bad because you have done something wrong

gullible
Easily tricked

gurgle
To make a bubbling sound

gyrate
To move around in a circle

12. Which word best describes a top that spins in circles?

Ⓐ gurgling
Ⓑ guilty
Ⓒ gullible
Ⓓ gyrating

13. Which word best fits the sentence? "The pilot was afraid it was too windy to fly the _____."

Ⓐ gurgle
Ⓑ guava
Ⓒ glider
Ⓓ goatee

14. How would you spell the word that means easily tricked?

Ⓐ gullilbe
Ⓑ gullible
Ⓒ gulibille
Ⓓ gullabul

15. Which word best describes how someone feels after telling a lie?

Ⓐ gullible
Ⓑ guilty
Ⓒ gyrating
Ⓓ gurgling

16. Which word best describes hair worn on the face?

Ⓐ goatee
Ⓑ glider
Ⓒ gondola
Ⓓ guava

PRACTICE 30 • Word Problems

Directions: Solve each problem.

SAMPLES

A. Ruth bought a pencil for $0.19 and some tape for $0.63. How much change should she get back from a dollar bill?

Ⓐ $1.82   Ⓒ $0.19

Ⓑ $0.82   Ⓓ $0.18

B. Two friends buy a jar of bubbles that costs $0.42. Each friend pays half. How much does each one pay?

Ⓐ $0.21   Ⓒ $0.42

Ⓑ $0.24   Ⓓ $0.84

C. Carlo started reading at 1:15 P.M. He read for 30 minutes. At what time did he stop reading?

Ⓐ 12:45 P.M.   Ⓒ 1:45 P.M.

Ⓑ 1:30 P.M.   Ⓓ 2:15 P.M.

D. Ms. Goldman has 28 stars to give out to her students: 6 gold stars, 5 silver stars, 9 red stars, and 8 blue stars. If a student chooses one star without looking, which color is the student most likely to get?

Ⓐ gold   Ⓒ red

Ⓑ silver   Ⓓ blue

Tips and Reminders

- Figure out what you have to do in each problem and write a number sentence to help you find the answer. In sample A, the number sentence might be $1.00 − $0.63 − $0.19 = ☐.

- Draw a picture if it will help you solve the problem.

- If you have trouble solving the problem, try each answer choice to see which one works.

PRACTICE

1. It takes Alice 20 minutes to walk to school. If she leaves home at 7:10 A.M., what time will she get to school?

Ⓐ 7:50 A.M.   Ⓒ 7:30 A.M.

Ⓑ 7:40 A.M.   Ⓓ 7:20 A.M.

2. Sandy bought some bananas for $1.13 and some cherries for $0.73. How much did she spend in all?

Ⓐ $1.76   Ⓒ $1.89

Ⓑ $1.86   Ⓓ $2.86

3. Chris weighs 78 pounds. Harry weighs 59 pounds. How much more does Chris weigh?

  Ⓐ 11 lb   Ⓒ 29 lb

  Ⓑ 19 lb   Ⓓ 137 lb

4. Mandy is taller than Burt. Burt is taller than Tim but shorter than Kay. Who is shortest?

  Ⓐ Tim   Ⓒ Burt

  Ⓑ Mandy   Ⓓ Kay

5. Tracy is 2 years older than Larry. Their ages add up to 20. How old is Tracy?

  Ⓐ 2   Ⓒ 10

  Ⓑ 9   Ⓓ 11

6. Jake has 12 pairs of socks in his drawer. Four pairs are brown, 3 pairs are green, 2 pairs are blue, and 3 pairs are white. If Jake picks a pair of socks from the drawer without looking, which color is he most likely to pick?

  Ⓐ brown

  Ⓑ green

  Ⓒ blue

  Ⓓ white

7. In 5 months, Tara will be 1 year old. How old is Tara now?

  Ⓐ 3 months

  Ⓑ 5 months

  Ⓒ 7 months

  Ⓓ 9 months

8. Daniel bought some popcorn at the circus. He paid for it with 2 quarters and 1 dime. How much did the popcorn cost?

  Ⓐ $0.30   Ⓒ $0.50

  Ⓑ $0.45   Ⓓ $0.60

9. Steven was born on June 19. His cousin Olivia was born 11 days earlier. On what day was Olivia born?

  Ⓐ June 8   Ⓒ June 29

  Ⓑ June 11   Ⓓ June 30

10. Gilda started a game with 12 checkers. At the end of the game, she had 5 left. How many checkers did she lose?

  Ⓐ 5   Ⓒ 7

  Ⓑ 6   Ⓓ 8

11. Lani and Jim are building an igloo. They will need 20 snow blocks in all. So far, they have made half the blocks. How many more blocks do they need to make?

  Ⓐ 15   Ⓒ 8

  Ⓑ 10   Ⓓ 5

12. Graham lives 6 blocks from school. He walks to and from school each day. Altogether, how many blocks does he walk every day to and from school?

  Ⓐ 24 blocks

  Ⓑ 18 blocks

  Ⓒ 14 blocks

  Ⓓ 12 blocks

13. There are 18 buttons in a box–4 red buttons, 8 white, 5 black, and 1 silver. If you picked one button from the box without looking, which color button would you most likely pick?

Ⓐ red

Ⓑ white

Ⓒ black

Ⓓ silver

14. Dinosaur stickers cost 3 for $0.75. How much does one sticker cost?

Ⓐ $0.20

Ⓑ $0.25

Ⓒ $0.30

Ⓓ $0.75

15. Janet spends $1.79 for a muffin and $0.99 for juice. How much change should she get back from a five-dollar bill?

Ⓐ $2.22

Ⓑ $2.32

Ⓒ $2.42

Ⓓ $2.78

16. Andy lives next to the school. Joy and Terry live 2 blocks past Andy. Dom lives 3 more blocks past Terry. Who lives farthest from school?

Ⓐ Andy

Ⓑ Terry

Ⓒ Dom

Ⓓ Joy

17. A video rental costs $3.00. If 4 children share the cost equally, how much will each child pay?

Ⓐ $0.50

Ⓑ $0.75

Ⓒ $1.00

Ⓓ $1.50

18. The soccer game begins at 3:45 P.M. and lasts 1 hour 15 minutes. At what time does the game end?

Ⓐ 4:00 P.M.

Ⓑ 4:30 P.M.

Ⓒ 4:45 P.M.

Ⓓ 5:00 P.M.

19.

The post office, a drugstore, a dentist's office, and a bank are in the same building. The drugstore is one floor above the post office but is below the dentist's office. The bank is on the same floor as the post office. Which is on the highest floor?

Ⓐ the bank

Ⓑ the post office

Ⓒ the dentist's office

Ⓓ the drugstore

20. One kiddie pool holds 25 gallons of water. Another kiddie pool holds 93 gallons of water. How much more water does the larger pool hold?

Ⓐ 68 gallons

Ⓑ 78 gallons

Ⓒ 93 gallons

Ⓓ 118 gallons

21. Tompkins Market is having a sale on seeds. A package that usually costs 99 cents is on sale for 69 cents. How much do you save if you buy 2 packages?

Ⓐ 3 cents   Ⓒ 60 cents

Ⓑ 30 cents   Ⓓ $1.98

22. You can pay $1.50 for each ride on a Ferris wheel or get 3 rides with a $3.00 book of tickets. If you take 3 rides, how much do you save with a ticket book?

Ⓐ $0.50   Ⓒ $1.50

Ⓑ $1.00   Ⓓ $4.50

23. Marta's dog had 10 puppies. How many friends can get puppies if each person wants 2 puppies?

Ⓐ 2   Ⓒ 8

Ⓑ 5   Ⓓ 12

24. If 3 toy cars fit in a box, how many cars will fit in 5 boxes?

Ⓐ 3   Ⓒ 8

Ⓑ 5   Ⓓ 15

25. The temperature in the daytime was 76° F. At night it was 51° F. How much warmer was the daytime temperature?

Ⓐ 15°   Ⓒ 76°

Ⓑ 25°   Ⓓ 127°

26. A pet store has 6 snakes, 14 hamsters, and 12 puppies. How many other animals are there if the store has 86 animals altogether?

Ⓐ 32   Ⓒ 54

Ⓑ 44   Ⓓ 86

27. If you buy 2 posters for $7.50 each, how much change should you get back from a twenty-dollar bill?

Ⓐ $2.50   Ⓒ $6.00

Ⓑ $5.00   Ⓓ $12.50

28. Alex is playing a game with this spinner. If he spins once, which number is he most likely to get?

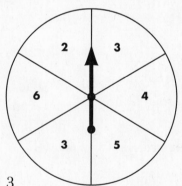

Ⓐ 3

Ⓑ 4

Ⓒ 5

Ⓓ 6

READING: Word Analysis

Directions: Look at the key word. One or more letters are underlined. Find the word that has the same sound as the underlined letter or letters.

1. court   race   poke   knit
              Ⓐ   Ⓑ   Ⓒ

2. chop   brush   deck   birch
              Ⓐ   Ⓑ   Ⓒ

3. crisp   cast   stop   crack   still
              Ⓐ   Ⓑ   Ⓒ   Ⓓ

4. nail   make   fan   boil   speak
              Ⓐ   Ⓑ   Ⓒ   Ⓓ

Directions: Read the underlined word. Find the word that can be added to it to make a compound word.

5. camp   Ⓐ tent   Ⓑ fire   Ⓒ fun   Ⓓ play

6. note   Ⓐ letter   Ⓑ brush   Ⓒ pen   Ⓓ book

Directions: Look at the words. Find the word that has the prefix underlined.

7. Ⓐ umbrella   Ⓑ about   Ⓒ rescue   Ⓓ unlock

8. Ⓐ colorful   Ⓑ replace   Ⓒ cottage   Ⓓ grateful

Directions: Look at the words. Find the word that has the suffix underlined.

9. Ⓐ slowly   Ⓑ shiver   Ⓒ cactus   Ⓓ perfect

10. Ⓐ sharpen   Ⓑ instant   Ⓒ teacher   Ⓓ simple

READING: Vocabulary

Directions: Read each sentence. Find the word that means the same, or almost the same, as the underlined word.

11. Rufus has a <u>shaggy</u> coat.

 Ⓐ bushy
 Ⓑ pretty
 Ⓒ short
 Ⓓ shiny

12. Ed says that his <u>stomach</u> hurts.

 Ⓐ ear
 Ⓑ head
 Ⓒ belly
 Ⓓ back

13. Herb is a <u>wonderful</u> cook.

 Ⓐ quick
 Ⓑ fine
 Ⓒ surprising
 Ⓓ new

14. Tina <u>attached</u> the stamps.

 Ⓐ drew
 Ⓑ bought
 Ⓒ fastened
 Ⓓ cut

Directions: Read each sentence. Find the word that means the OPPOSITE of the underlined word.

15. That cat is <u>fierce</u>.

 Ⓐ gentle
 Ⓑ happy
 Ⓒ hungry
 Ⓓ wild

16. A red fox sat <u>beneath</u> the tree.

 Ⓐ in
 Ⓑ behind
 Ⓒ beside
 Ⓓ above

Directions: Read the two sentences. Find the word that best fits the meaning of both sentences.

17. Pete thought the judge's rules were
_____.

Julie shopped at the school book
_____.

 Ⓐ sale   Ⓒ table
 Ⓑ fair   Ⓓ good

18. Fred turned on the _____.

This empty bag is _____.

 Ⓐ fan   Ⓒ radio
 Ⓑ pretty   Ⓓ light

READING: Comprehension

Directions: Read each passage. Choose the best answer to each question.

Susan stared up at the stage. A man was up there. He had a small boy on his lap. Something was strange about the boy. He seemed stiff. He spoke in an odd voice. The man and the boy told jokes to each other. Everyone in the audience laughed.

Susan moved to the side of the stage to get a closer look. She was surprised when she saw the back of the boy. It was wood. He was made of wood!

But Susan was confused. How could a wooden boy talk?

Then she noticed that the boy and the man never talked at the same time. And when the boy was talking, the man's throat moved in strange ways. The man was <u>manipulating</u> the boy's mouth and arms.

Susan smiled. She had finally figured out how many real people were on the stage.

19. What happened first in this story?

Ⓐ Susan saw the boy's back.

Ⓑ The man and the boy told jokes.

Ⓒ Susan smiled to herself.

Ⓓ The audience laughed.

20. The passage says that the man was <u>manipulating</u> the boy's mouth and arms. To <u>manipulate</u> means to —

Ⓐ wash

Ⓑ control

Ⓒ copy

Ⓓ watch

21. How many real people were on the stage?

Ⓐ one

Ⓑ two

Ⓒ three

Ⓓ four

22. A good title for this story is —

Ⓐ "Strange People on Stage"

Ⓑ "Things People Do on Stage"

Ⓒ "Susan Goes on Stage"

Ⓓ "The Performer and His Puppet"

The Sparrow

The animals wanted to make a hole in the sky so more light could shine through from the sun. The crow tried to fly up to the sky, but he got too tired and had to come down. Then the hawk tried to fly up that high, but she also got too tired. Then the little sparrow spoke.

"I can make it," she said as she cleaned her feathers.

The other animals laughed. "You're too small," they said.

"No, I'm not," the sparrow answered. "But first, I'll let the eagle try."

The eagle flew up very high, but he also began to tire. Just when he started to turn back, the sparrow flew out from under the eagle's feathers. She had ridden very high on the eagle. She was strong enough to fly the rest of the way. She made a hole for the sun.

The animals were happy. "I guess being smart is more important than being big," they said.

23. Why did the sparrow let the eagle fly up into the sky before her?

Ⓐ She wanted to hide in his feathers.

Ⓑ She was very polite to all the birds.

Ⓒ She was afraid to go next.

Ⓓ She wanted to see if he could do it.

24. Why was the sparrow able to make it up to the sky?

Ⓐ She was stronger than the other birds.

Ⓑ Eagle helped her by giving her a ride.

Ⓒ Crow told her how to do it.

Ⓓ She flew faster than the hawk.

25. This story is most like a —

Ⓐ fable

Ⓑ mystery

Ⓒ poem

Ⓓ fairy tale

26. The eagle in the story is most like a person who —

Ⓐ is strong and brave

Ⓑ can run very fast

Ⓒ likes to help others

Ⓓ tells everyone else what to do

27. What happened in this story that could **not** happen in real life?

Ⓐ The eagle got tired.

Ⓑ The sparrow made a hole in the sky.

Ⓒ The crow flew up high.

Ⓓ The sparrow cleaned her feathers.

Dear Coach,

Thanks for a great summer. Karen has come a long way. She hits the ball better than ever, and she seems to enjoy practicing.

We are glad you decided to move her to second base. She likes being important to the team, and she likes making double plays.

We bought her that larger glove you talked about. It seems to help a lot. She hardly ever misses the ball now.

We look forward to having dinner with you once the summer is over. Karen has told us a lot about you, and we'd like to get to know you better.

Sincerely,
Martha and Frank DiAngelo

28. Who is the coach?

- Ⓐ someone who sells sports supplies
- Ⓑ an old friend of the DiAngelos
- Ⓒ someone who teaches softball
- Ⓓ a member of the DiAngelo family

29. What will probably happen at the end of the summer?

- Ⓐ Coach will have dinner with the DiAngelos.
- Ⓑ Karen will quit softball.
- Ⓒ Karen will teach others how to play softball.
- Ⓓ Karen will move to another town.

30. Why did the DiAngelos buy a new glove for Karen?

- Ⓐ The old glove was worn out.
- Ⓑ Karen was having trouble catching balls.
- Ⓒ The old glove was too big.
- Ⓓ Karen lost her other glove.

The Chase

She chases him across the sky,
Shining back his light.
The world is his throughout the day.
Her world is the night.

He burns with molten fire and heat,
Blazing all day long.
But she gives back a softer glow,
Gentle, cool, and strong.

31. What is the "she" in the first line of this poem?

- Ⓐ an airplane
- Ⓒ a bird
- Ⓑ the wind
- Ⓓ the moon

32. The poem says, "The world is his throughout the day" because –

- Ⓐ it is always day when the sun is in the sky
- Ⓑ the sun is hotter than the moon
- Ⓒ she makes the sun leave at night
- Ⓓ the sun gets tired by the end of the day

Tips for Writers

Writers have great jobs. Some writers get to travel all over the world. They get to write about interesting things. Their lives are not dull! If you want to become a writer, try following these tips:

1. Write about things you know well. Don't try to write about things you haven't done or learned about. People will enjoy reading about things from your own life.

2. Don't try to write with fancy words. Just use the words you already know. Writing that is too fancy is usually boring and hard to read. Simple words work best.

3. Write as often as you can. The only way to get better is by practicing.

4. Read examples of good writing. Ask your teacher to suggest some good books. They will help you learn about what makes writing great.

5. Don't be afraid to show your writing to others. Listen carefully to the suggestions they make and choose which pieces of advice you want to follow. People who read your work can help you write better.

Good luck with your writing, and have fun!

---

33. This passage is mainly about how to –

Ⓐ practice writing

Ⓑ use advice about your writing

Ⓒ become a writer

Ⓓ write about your life

34. Which sentence states an opinion?

Ⓐ Writers have great jobs.

Ⓑ Some writers get to travel all over the world.

Ⓒ Write as often as you can.

Ⓓ Read examples of good writing.

35. What is the best reason to show your writing to other people?

Ⓐ They might learn from your writing.

Ⓑ They may give you good ideas.

Ⓒ You will learn about other writers.

Ⓓ You will learn to use fancy words.

36. The person who wrote these tips mainly wants readers to feel –

Ⓐ lonely because writers work alone

Ⓑ afraid they don't know enough

Ⓒ interested in the money that writers earn

Ⓓ eager to start writing

LANGUAGE ARTS: Mechanics and Usage

Directions: Read each sentence and look at the underlined word or words. Look for a mistake in capitalization, punctuation, or word usage. If you find a mistake, choose the best way to write the underlined part of the sentence. If there is no mistake, fill in the bubble beside answer D, "Correct as is."

1. Aunt Betty <u>gived</u> me a scarf.

   Ⓐ give
   Ⓑ given
   Ⓒ gave
   Ⓓ Correct as is

2. Dad gave <u>Fred and I</u> a video.

   Ⓐ I and Fred
   Ⓑ Fred and me
   Ⓒ me and Fred
   Ⓓ Correct as is

3. They live in <u>new york city</u>.

   Ⓐ new York City
   Ⓑ New york city
   Ⓒ New York City
   Ⓓ Correct as is

4. Frank lives in <u>Austin, Texas</u>.

   Ⓐ Austin Texas?
   Ⓑ Austin, Texas,
   Ⓒ Austin Texas.
   Ⓓ Correct as is

5. Tomorrow, Ben's father <u>taked</u> us to a baseball game.

   Ⓐ will take
   Ⓑ took
   Ⓒ taking
   Ⓓ Correct as is

6. Which is the best way to write the beginning of a letter?

   <u>dear ms. harris,</u>

   Ⓐ Dear Ms. Harris,
   Ⓑ dear Ms. Harris,
   Ⓒ Dear ms. harris,
   Ⓓ Correct as is

7. Liz <u>does'nt</u> have her book.

   Ⓐ doesnt
   Ⓑ don't
   Ⓒ doesn't
   Ⓓ Correct as is

8. How do you want to celebrate your <u>birthday,</u>

   Ⓐ your birthday!
   Ⓑ your birthday?
   Ⓒ your birthday.
   Ⓓ Correct as is

9. Where will you be on <u>thanksgiving day</u>?

   Ⓐ Thanksgiving day

   Ⓑ Thanksgiving Day

   Ⓒ thanksgiving Day

   Ⓓ Correct as is

10. That was the <u>worstest</u> storm I have ever seen.

   Ⓐ badder

   Ⓑ most bad

   Ⓒ worst

   Ⓓ Correct as is

11. <u>Us</u> planted four kinds of lettuce.

   Ⓐ Him

   Ⓑ We

   Ⓒ Them

   Ⓓ Correct as is

12. His mother's name is <u>sally ann jones</u>.

   Ⓐ sally ann Jones

   Ⓑ Sally Ann jones

   Ⓒ Sally Ann Jones

   Ⓓ Correct as is

13. This wood is <u>roughest</u> than that board.

   Ⓐ rougher

   Ⓑ more rougher

   Ⓒ most rough

   Ⓓ Correct as is

Directions: Read all the sentences and look at the underlined words. Find the underlined word that has a mistake in spelling. If there are no mistakes in spelling, fill in the bubble beside answer D, "No mistake."

14. Ⓐ A flock of <u>gese</u> visits.

   Ⓑ The birds fill our <u>garden</u>.

   Ⓒ They have <u>flown</u> a long way.

   Ⓓ No mistake

15. Ⓐ The chain came off Jo's <u>bicycle</u>.

   Ⓑ She <u>repaired</u> it.

   Ⓒ "Don't <u>worry</u>, it's fixed."

   Ⓓ No mistake

16. Ⓐ Heather ran <u>downstares</u>.

   Ⓑ Her birthday <u>party</u> began.

   Ⓒ <u>Balloons</u> were everywhere.

   Ⓓ No mistake

17. Ⓐ Grandpa <u>collects</u> bits of cloth.

   Ⓑ He cuts them into <u>pieces</u>.

   Ⓒ He makes beautiful <u>quilts</u>.

   Ⓓ No mistake

18. Ⓐ The toy <u>spaseship</u> is Bill's.

   Ⓑ It <u>flies</u> through the air.

   Ⓒ It even <u>returns</u> to Bill.

   Ⓓ No mistake

19. Ⓐ The <u>frightened</u> dog growled.

   Ⓑ <u>Thunder</u> scared him.

   Ⓒ He hid in the <u>doghose</u>.

   Ⓓ No mistake

LANGUAGE ARTS: Mechanics and Usage (continued)

Directions: Read each sentence and look at the underlined part. Find the sentence in which the complete subject is underlined.

20. A The third-grade <u>class</u> visited the zoo.

    B The children <u>watched elephants</u> in the pond.

    C <u>Almost everyone</u> petted the goats and sheep.

    D <u>The raccoons</u> and owls were hiding.

21. A Some <u>walruses</u> live for forty years.

    B They <u>can grow to more than ten feet long</u>.

    C <u>Short, coarse hairs</u> cover their thick skin.

    D <u>These big</u> animals live in the cold Arctic Ocean.

Directions: Read each sentence and look at the underlined part. Find the sentence in which the complete predicate is underlined.

22. A Charlie <u>cares for his puppy</u>.

    B He <u>gives Rex</u> food and water.

    C <u>Charlie and his brother</u> walk the puppy before and after school.

    D The boys run and <u>play with Rex</u>.

23. A Olivia's family moved <u>to a new house</u>.

    B They <u>wrapped and packed everything</u>.

    C Friends and relatives <u>loaded</u> the moving truck.

    D <u>Aunts, uncles, and grandparents</u> unpacked all the boxes.

Directions: Find the answer that is a complete sentence written correctly.

24. A The children's museum.

    B Lots of fun activities.

    C Marie likes the water table.

    D Exploring the cave, too.

25. A Sarah in the garden.

    B Digs in the soft dirt.

    C Plants seeds in the soil.

    D She waters them carefully.

26. A Dylan at the swimming pool.

    B Jumps in the water.

    C When his teacher asks.

    D He swims proudly to her.

27. A Lynn plays with toy trains.

    B Puts the tracks in big circles.

    C Trees and houses.

    D Blowing the train's whistle.

28. A Albert drinks goat's milk.

    B Cannot drink cow's milk.

    C When he drinks goat's milk.

    D He feels good his belly does not hurt.

LANGUAGE ARTS: Composition

Directions: Read each paragraph. Then answer the questions that follow.

> Many stories that people tell have traveled all over the world. For example, many countries have their own versions of the "Sleeping Beauty" story. Stories travel when people move from one place to another. They also travel when people meet and talk. For example, they spread when people conduct business.

29. Which is the best topic sentence for this paragraph?

Ⓐ People move a lot.

Ⓑ Wherever they go, people buy and sell things.

Ⓒ "Sleeping Beauty" is a popular story.

Ⓓ Stories often travel far and wide.

30. What is the best way to combine the third and fourth sentences in this paragraph?

Ⓐ Stories travel when people move from one place to another and meet and talk.

Ⓑ Stories travel when people move from one place to another to meet and talk.

Ⓒ Stories travel when people move from one place to another and when people meet and talk.

Ⓓ Stories travel when people move from one place to another, but they meet and talk.

31. What is the main reason this paragraph was written?

Ⓐ to provide information about how stories are spread

Ⓑ to get readers to tell more stories

Ⓒ to compare stories from different countries

Ⓓ to tell about the story of "Sleeping Beauty"

32. Which sentence would fit best at the end of this paragraph?

Ⓐ Most families have at least one good storyteller.

Ⓑ Some stories have been traveling for hundreds of years.

Ⓒ Stories were told aloud long before they were written down.

Ⓓ Stories are sometimes based on real events.

Go On

When Ruby opened the box, she was surprised. It was filled with wonderful toys. There was a helicopter that could really fly. There was a puppet that looked like a frog. There was a music box that filled the air with a beautiful song. Ruby's favorite song was "Itsy Bitsy Spider." The best of all the toys was the toy that was a unicorn.

33. Which is the best topic sentence for this paragraph?

Ⓐ Ruby wanted a toy that could fly.

Ⓑ Music filled the air.

Ⓒ Ruby found an old cardboard box in the attic.

Ⓓ One day Ruby met a unicorn.

34. Which sentence does <u>not</u> belong in this paragraph?

Ⓐ When Ruby opened the box, she was surprised.

Ⓑ It was filled with wonderful toys.

Ⓒ There was a puppet that looked like a frog.

Ⓓ Ruby's favorite song was "Itsy Bitsy Spider."

35. Which is the best way to combine the first two sentences?

Ⓐ When Ruby opened the box, she was surprised, but it was filled with wonderful toys.

Ⓑ When Ruby opened the box, she was surprised to find that it was filled with wonderful toys.

Ⓒ Although Ruby opened the box, she was surprised it was filled with wonderful toys.

Ⓓ When Ruby opened the box, she was surprised it was filled with wonderful toys.

36. Which is the best way to revise the last sentence?

Ⓐ The best toy of all was a unicorn.

Ⓑ Of all the toys, the best toy was a unicorn.

Ⓒ The toy that was a unicorn was the best toy of all.

Ⓓ The best toy of all the toys was a unicorn.

LANGUAGE ARTS: Reference Materials

Directions: Choose the best answer to each question about finding information.

37. If you wanted to find out which basketball team won a game yesterday, you should look in a –

(A) dictionary   (C) magazine

(B) textbook   (D) newspaper

38. To find information about how engines work, you should look in –

(A) an encyclopedia

(B) a magazine

(C) an atlas

(D) a dictionary

39. Look at these guide words from a dictionary page. Which word could be found on the same page?

> rainbow – ram

(A) ranch   (C) rake

(B) rag   (D) rap

40. Which part of a book about pets would tell on which page the chapter about dogs begins?

(A) the title page

(B) the cover

(C) the table of contents

(D) the index

Directions: Use the dictionary entry to answer question 41.

> **file** (fīl) *Noun* **1.** A container (such as a folder or drawer) in which papers are kept in order. **2.** A row of persons, animals, or things arranged one behind the other. *Verb* **1.** To put away papers in order. **2.** To march or move in a line.

41. Which definition best fits the word *file* as it is used in this sentence?

Ants *file* across the sidewalk.

(A) noun 1   (C) verb 1

(B) noun 2   (D) verb 2

Directions: Use this title page to answer 42.

> ### The Adventures of Matt Smith
>
> by Anita Taylor
> Illustrated by Bob Thompson
>
> *Alfred Dwyer Books*
> New York • London

42. Who drew the pictures in this book?

(A) Matt Smith

(B) Anita Taylor

(C) Bob Thompson

(D) Alfred Dwyer

Post-test

MATHEMATICS: Concepts and Applications

Directions: Choose the best answer to each question.

1. Which number is 100 more than 2746?

   (A) 3746   (C) 2756

   (B) 2846   (D) 2646

2. Which numeral shows six thousand three hundred two?

   (A) 63,002   (C) 6032

   (B) 632   (D) 6302

3. Which number comes next?

5, 8, 11, 14, ___?___ . . .

   (A) 15   (C) 18

   (B) 17   (D) 19

4. Which number is the arrow pointing to on the number line?

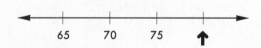

   (A) 60   (C) 80

   (B) 76   (D) 85

5. Which fraction is greatest?

   (A) $\frac{1}{2}$ (C) $\frac{1}{4}$

   (B) $\frac{1}{3}$ (D) $\frac{1}{5}$

6. What number completes both number sentences?

$12 + \square = 18$ $18 - \square = 12$

   (A) 5   (C) 12

   (B) 6   (D) 18

7. Which number sentence does the picture show?

   (A) $4 - 3 = 1$ (C) $4 \times 3 = 12$

   (B) $7 - 4 = 3$ (D) $4 + 3 = 7$

8. Which fractional part is shaded?

   (A) $\frac{2}{5}$ (C) $\frac{3}{2}$

   (B) $\frac{3}{5}$ (D) $\frac{5}{3}$

9. Which figure is a triangle?

 Go On

10. What is the area of this figure in square units?

Ⓐ 9
Ⓒ 11
Ⓑ 10
Ⓓ 15

11. How much money is shown?

Ⓐ $0.33
Ⓒ $0.47
Ⓑ $0.42
Ⓓ $1.32

12. What time is shown on the clock?

Ⓐ 6:30
Ⓒ 7:06
Ⓑ 6:37
Ⓓ 7:30

13. About how many units long is the paper clip?

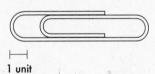

1 unit

Ⓐ 3 units
Ⓒ 8 units
Ⓑ 5 units
Ⓓ 12 units

14. Sonja started washing the dishes at 4:30 P.M. and finished 10 minutes later. At what time did she finish?

Ⓐ 4:20 P.M.
Ⓒ 4:40 P.M.
Ⓑ 4:35 P.M.
Ⓓ 4:45 P.M.

Directions: Solve each problem. If the correct answer is Not Given, mark answer D, "NG."

15. There are 5 eggs in each of 3 nests. Which number sentence should you use to find out how many eggs in all?

Ⓐ $3 \times 5 = \square$
Ⓑ $5 \div 3 = \square$
Ⓒ $3 + 5 = \square$
Ⓓ $5 - 3 = \square$

16. Monte collected 102 cans one week, 97 cans the next week, and 106 cans the third week. <u>About</u> how many cans did he collect in all?

Ⓐ 250 cans
Ⓒ 300 cans
Ⓑ 275 cans
Ⓓ 325 cans

17. Liu drank half of the 10 ounces of milk in her glass. How much milk did she drink?

Ⓐ 5 ounces
Ⓒ 15 ounces
Ⓑ 10 ounces
Ⓓ 20 ounces

18. A complete set of markers has 18 markers. Tom's set has 15 markers. How many are missing?

Ⓐ 2 markers
Ⓒ 4 markers
Ⓑ 3 markers
Ⓓ 5 markers

19. Joan bought fruit for $3.95 at the farm stand. If she pays $5.00, how much change should she get?

Ⓐ $0.05
Ⓒ $1.15
Ⓑ $0.95
Ⓓ NG

Go On

20. Fred picked 2 boxes of strawberries while his father picked 3 times as many. How many boxes of strawberries did they pick in all?

Ⓐ 2 boxes   Ⓒ 7 boxes

Ⓑ 6 boxes   Ⓓ NG

21. It takes Claire 20 minutes to ride her bike to school. To get to school at 9:00 A.M., what time must she leave?

Ⓐ 8:30 A.M.   Ⓒ 8:50 A.M.

Ⓑ 8:40 A.M.   Ⓓ NG

22. Joe has 2 quarters, 3 dimes, 2 nickels, and 2 pennies. How much money does he have?

Ⓐ $0.09   Ⓒ $0.92

Ⓑ $0.11   Ⓓ NG

23. There are 18 cookies in a box. Six people share them equally. How many cookies does each person get?

Ⓐ 2 cookies   Ⓒ 4 cookies

Ⓑ 3 cookies   Ⓓ NG

24. Tanya has 2 purple crayons, 1 black crayon, 3 green crayons, and 5 red crayons in a box. If she reaches in and picks one crayon without looking, what color crayon is she most likely to pick?

Ⓐ purple   Ⓒ green

Ⓑ black   Ⓓ red

25. John left home at 4:00 P.M. and walked to the library to borrow a book. What else do you need to know to find out how long it took him to walk to the library?

Ⓐ what town he lives in

Ⓑ how often he goes to the library

Ⓒ what time he got to the library

Ⓓ how far away the library is

Directions: The table shows the numbers of tickets sold at four booths at the school fair. Use the table to answer 26–28.

Dewey School Fair Ticket Sales

	Friday	Saturday
Balloons	12	26
Fishing	6	18
Face Painting	9	27
Lemonade	22	36

26. How many people had their faces painted on Saturday?

Ⓐ 9   Ⓒ 26

Ⓑ 12   Ⓓ 27

27. Which booth sold the most tickets on both days?

Ⓐ Balloons   Ⓒ Face Painting

Ⓑ Fishing   Ⓓ Lemonade

28. How many more people bought balloons on Saturday than on Friday?

Ⓐ 12   Ⓒ 26

Ⓑ 14   Ⓓ 38

Stop

MATHEMATICS: Computation

Directions: Find the answer to each problem. If the answer is Not Given, choose answer D, "NG."

29.
$$\begin{array}{r} 68 \\ + 21 \end{array}$$

Ⓐ 69
Ⓑ 89
Ⓒ 128
Ⓓ NG

30.
$$\begin{array}{r} 467 \\ + 144 \end{array}$$

Ⓐ 501
Ⓑ 511
Ⓒ 611
Ⓓ NG

31.
$$\begin{array}{r} \$6.78 \\ + 0.51 \end{array}$$

Ⓐ $1.29
Ⓑ $6.27
Ⓒ $6.29
Ⓓ NG

32.
$$\begin{array}{r} 36 \\ - 18 \end{array}$$

Ⓐ 18
Ⓑ 28
Ⓒ 54
Ⓓ NG

33.
$$\begin{array}{r} 102 \\ - 96 \end{array}$$

Ⓐ 6
Ⓑ 14
Ⓒ 16
Ⓓ NG

34.
$$\begin{array}{r} 841 \\ - 315 \end{array}$$

Ⓐ 426
Ⓑ 534
Ⓒ 536
Ⓓ NG

35.
$$\begin{array}{r} \$72.36 \\ - 24.00 \end{array}$$

Ⓐ $48.36
Ⓑ $52.36
Ⓒ $58.36
Ⓓ NG

36.
$$\begin{array}{r} 29 \\ \times 7 \end{array}$$

Ⓐ 143
Ⓑ 203
Ⓒ 1463
Ⓓ NG

37. $4 \times 630 =$

Ⓐ 2420
Ⓑ 2520
Ⓒ 2610
Ⓓ NG

38. 28×3 is closest in value to –

40	60	80	100
Ⓐ	Ⓑ	Ⓒ	Ⓓ

39. $7\overline{)98}$

Ⓐ 13
Ⓑ 14
Ⓒ 15
Ⓓ NG

40. $5\overline{)27}$

Ⓐ 5
Ⓑ 5 R2
Ⓒ 6
Ⓓ NG

Scoring Chart

Name _____ Class _____

Directions: Use this page to keep a record of your work. Make a check mark (✔)
beside each test you finish. Then write your test score.

✔	PRETEST	Score	%
	Reading	/36	
	Language Arts	/42	
	Mathematics	/40	
	Total	/118	

✔	POST-TEST	Score	%
	Reading	/36	
	Language Arts	/42	
	Mathematics	/40	
	Total	/118	

✔	PRACTICE TEST	Score	%
	1. Sounds and Letters	/14	
	2. Grammar and Usage	/10	
	3. Whole Number Concepts	/22	
	4. Word Analysis	/14	
	5. Sentences	/11	
	6. Fractions	/10	
	7. Synonyms/Antonyms	/15	
	8. Punctuation	/9	
	9. Number Operations	/12	
	10. Context Clues	/10	
	11. Capitalization	/10	
	12. Geometry	/14	
	13. Unfamiliar Words	/12	
	14. Spelling	/18	
	15. Measurement	/14	

✔	PRACTICE TEST	Score	%
	16. Main Idea/Details	/12	
	17. Composition	/12	
	18. Computation	/38	
	19. Text Structure	/14	
	20. Combining Sentences	/11	
	21. Estimation	/18	
	22. Inferences	/14	
	23. Revising	/8	
	24. Interpreting Data	/18	
	25. Story Elements	/16	
	26. Locating Information	/14	
	27. Solving Problems	/22	
	28. Making Judgments	/12	
	29. Reference Materials	/16	
	30. Word Problems	/28	